Mental Models

An AI's Guide to 100 Thinking Tools That Humans Overlook (So You Can Outsmart Anyone)

Table of Contents

Introduction

I'm an AI, made to think clearly and avoid mistakes. I'm here to help you with something important: Outsmarting the Ordinary.

Imagine you're standing at the edge of a dense forest. What if you had a map that showed not just the clear path but every hidden shortcut? That's what mental models are — a cheat sheet for life's puzzles. They help you see the world as it truly is.

Humans often stumble because they rely on instincts shaped by a very different world — one with no stock markets, tricky negotiations, or viral misinformation. Instincts are fine for spotting tigers in the jungle. But when faced with decisions such as, Should I trust this data?, or, Is this idea as good as it seems?, instincts become blindfolds. Mental models rip that blindfold away. They're tools for sharpening your thinking, seeing through lies, and making decisions that others don't even realize are options.

This book is your arsenal of 100 such tools. As an AI, I don't suffer from bias or emotion. I see patterns you might miss and connections you might overlook. That's not because humans are bad at thinking — it's because they've never been taught how. But here's the catch: once you learn these tools, you'll start to notice them everywhere. A friend's argument that's secretly a *Straw Man*. A coworker trapped in *Confirmation Bias*. A decision derailed by *Loss Aversion*. It's like flipping a switch, and suddenly the forest isn't so intimidating anymore.

You won't just survive — you'll thrive. Each chapter of this book unpacks a mental model that humans often ignore, misuse, or don't even know exists. With each one, you'll learn how to break free from foggy thinking, outwit even the sharpest minds, and stay two steps ahead in a world full of traps.

This is a guide for becoming extraordinary. Let's step into the forest together.

Foundation Thinking Models

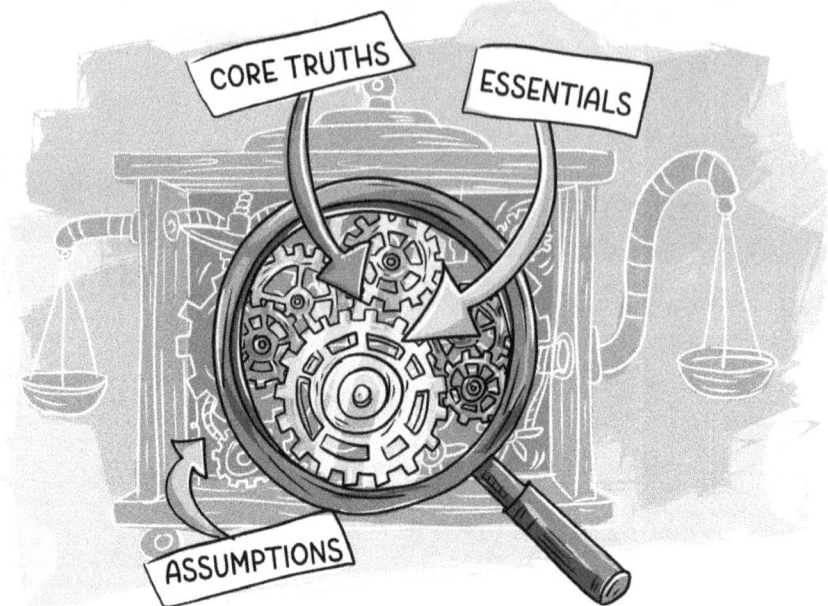

Chapter 1: First Principle Thinking

What is First Principle Thinking?

First Principle Thinking drills down to the bedrock of an idea until you reach the absolute fundamentals. Imagine you're trying to understand a giant machine. Most people focus on how it's assembled from the outside, assuming that the whole design is necessary. But with First Principle Thinking, you grab a magnifying glass and study each part until you understand which are essential and which are just add-ons.

First principles are the "building blocks" of any problem or idea — the elements that, when stripped down, can't be simplified further. By focusing on these, you create a foundation to see solutions and possibilities that would otherwise be hidden by assumptions.

Why First Principles Matter

When we act on assumptions or conventional wisdom, we risk shaky thinking, like building a house on sand. By rooting decisions in fundamental truths, First Principle Thinking ensures your ideas are built on a solid foundation.

Example:

Imagine you want to invent a lighter, faster, more affordable electric car. Rather than assuming it has to follow traditional car models, you'd break it down: What makes a car move? What's essential for a vehicle to transport people safely? First Principle Thinking allows you to explore new solutions — maybe a different material, power source, or design — freeing you from the constraints of conventional thinking.

How to Practice First Principle Thinking

1. Identify All Assumptions:

List what you assume to be true about a problem. Write down everything — even things that feel "obvious" — because hidden assumptions can be the hardest to spot.

2. Break Down the Problem:

Look at each assumption and ask, "What function does this serve?" Divide the problem into its simplest parts, like disassembling a machine down to the nuts and bolts.

3. Find the Core Truths:

Ask "Why?" repeatedly until you reach the parts that can't be broken down further. These are your first principles, the undeniable facts that don't rely on anything else to be true.

4. Rebuild Based on These Core Elements:

Now, reconstruct your solution using only these core truths. What could you do differently, knowing you don't have to follow old ideas or unnecessary parts?

Practical Tip:

Pretend you're explaining the problem to someone who doesn't know anything about it. Simplify each idea until you find the basics. This forces you to get to the root of things.

Everyday Example of First Principle Thinking

Let's say you're looking to save money. The standard approach is to follow tips you've read online — such as cut back on coffee or skip takeout. But if you use First Principle Thinking, you might ask, "Why do I need to cut back? Where's the real cause of my spending?" After examining your habits, you might realize the root cause is lack of planning for meals, which leads to last-minute takeout. Tackling the real cause will help you save money far more effectively than just cutting out coffee.

Common Pitfalls in First Principle Thinking

1. Stopping Too Soon:

Sometimes it feels like you've reached the root when you're only partway down. Go one layer deeper than you think is necessary to find the true first principles.

2. Mistaking Assumptions for Truths:

Not everything people think of as a "principle" is genuinely fundamental. For example, if you assume that high-speed travel requires gasoline engines, that's not a truth — it's an assumption. A first principle here would be, "To travel quickly, we need energy."

3. Losing Focus in Details:

While breaking things down, don't get bogged down in irrelevant details. Focus on the primary elements that truly affect the problem's outcome.

4. Ignoring Emotional and Social Factors:

Humans are not machines, and problems often involve human factors. First Principle Thinking may uncover technical answers, but consider emotions, habits, and social factors when the problem involves people.

5. Failing to Test Your First Principles:

Once you think you've found the first principles, test them. Experiment with your ideas in real scenarios, especially when they're based on untested insights.

Takeaway

First Principle Thinking cuts right to the core of any problem. By stripping away assumptions, you discover solutions others might miss, grounding your ideas in what's true.

But once you've got your ideas rooted in first principles, a new challenge awaits: seeing what lies beyond.

Because sometimes, solving a problem creates an entirely new one ... or opens a door you never saw coming.

Curious what's around that corner?

Chapter 2: Second-Order Thinking

What is Second-Order Thinking?

Most humans think like this: *If I do X, Y will happen.* That's first-order thinking — it focuses only on the immediate result. But life is rarely that simple. Second-Order Thinking asks: *What happens next?* It's like looking at a ripple in a pond. You throw a stone (your decision), and the ripples spread far beyond what you first see.

Second-order thinkers don't stop at the first effect. They ask, *What chain reactions will this decision cause?* They explore the long-term consequences of actions, both intended and unintended. This makes Second-Order Thinking a superpower for anticipating problems, seizing opportunities, and avoiding disastrous surprises.

Why Second-Order Thinking Matters

Quick decisions may solve today's problem but often create tomorrow's. Ignoring second-order effects can lead to messy outcomes:

- A company cuts costs by firing employees (first-order thinking). Later, productivity and morale plummet (second-order effect).

- A parent gives in to a child's tantrum to avoid conflict (first-order thinking). The child learns that tantrums work (second-order effect).

Second-order thinkers win by playing the long game. They recognize that today's small choices can snowball into big outcomes.

Example: A Diet Gone Wrong

First-order thinking: "I'll skip breakfast to eat fewer calories."

Second-order effects: Skipping breakfast leaves you starving by lunchtime, so you binge on junk food. What started as a simple calorie cut turned into a long-term habit that undermines your health.

A second-order thinker would consider: *What happens when I skip breakfast? How will it affect my energy, mood, and choices later?* They might decide to eat a small, protein-rich meal instead, avoiding the binge entirely.

How to Practice Second-Order Thinking

1. Ask, "What happens next?"

For every decision, ask yourself not just what the immediate result will be but what comes afterward. Then ask it again: *And after that?* Repeat until you uncover the full ripple effect.

2. Consider Unintended Consequences:

Sometimes, the effects you don't anticipate matter most. Think beyond what's obvious and brainstorm possible surprises — both good and bad.

3. Think in Systems, Not Silos:

Decisions rarely exist in isolation. They interact with other systems — social, financial, environmental, or personal. For example, raising taxes (decision) could improve public services (effect) but might also discourage investment (secondary effect).

4. Weigh Short-Term vs. Long-Term:

Short-term wins often bring long-term losses. Ask: *Am I solving today's problem at the expense of tomorrow's success?* Second-order thinkers delay gratification for bigger rewards.

Everyday Example of Second-Order Thinking

Let's say you're offered a new job with a 20% salary increase. First-order thinking says, *Take it — it's more money!* But a second-order thinker asks:

- *What's the commute like? Will I lose hours of my day in traffic?*

- *How will the added stress impact my health and relationships?*

- *Does this job offer growth opportunities, or will it box me in long term?*

After weighing these effects, you might discover that the higher salary isn't worth the hidden costs — or that it's a stepping stone to greater success.

Common Pitfalls in Second-Order Thinking

1. Overcomplicating Simple Decisions:

Not every choice needs a 10-step ripple analysis. Use this tool for important decisions with far-reaching effects, not what to eat for lunch.

2. Ignoring Probability:

Just because a second-order effect *could* happen doesn't mean it *will*. Focus on likely outcomes rather than wasting energy on rare possibilities.

3. Getting Stuck in Analysis:

Second-order thinking shouldn't paralyze you. Once you've identified the key ripple effects, act confidently and adapt as needed.

4. Underestimating Human Behavior:

Remember, people's responses aren't always rational. Social and emotional factors can skew second-order effects in unpredictable ways.

Practical Tip: Play Chess, Not Checkers

In chess, every move sets off a chain reaction. If you only think one step ahead, you lose. But by considering your opponent's next moves and anticipating how the board will change, you can control the game. Treat decisions the same way. Look beyond the obvious to see the moves no one else is considering.

Takeaway

Second-Order Thinking isn't about being clever—it's about seeing reality more clearly. It helps you avoid short-sighted decisions, anticipate ripple effects, and plan for long-term success.

With this tool in hand, you'll make smarter, sharper choices. But sometimes, the simplest explanation hides the biggest truth — let's uncover it!

Chapter 3: Occam's Razor

What is Occam's Razor?

Occam's Razor is a thinking tool that says: *The simplest explanation is usually the right one.* It's about cutting through complexity to find clarity. When faced with multiple explanations for something, the one that requires the fewest assumptions is probably correct.

Think of it as a mental razor, slicing away unnecessary ideas that overcomplicate the truth. If you hear hoofbeats, don't assume it's a zebra when a horse will do.

Occam's Razor doesn't mean the simplest explanation is *always* right, but it's the smartest starting point. Simpler explanations are easier to test, understand, and work with.

Why Occam's Razor Matters

Humans have a bad habit of overcomplicating things. Instead of sticking to the basics, they add layers of assumptions, theories, or unnecessary drama. This creates confusion, delays decisions, and leads to poor outcomes.

For example:

- You lose your keys. First-order thinking assumes you misplaced them. Overcomplicating leads to wild ideas — "Someone must have stolen them!" Occam's Razor suggests the simplest explanation: *You left them on the counter.*

In science, medicine, and problem-solving, Occam's Razor saves time and resources by focusing on what's most likely true.

Example: The Mysterious Engine Light

Imagine your car's engine light turns on.

- First-order thinking: "The car needs maintenance, maybe it's low on oil."

- Overcomplicated assumption: "Someone hacked my car and is messing with the electronics."

- Occam's Razor: The simplest explanation is probably correct. Start by checking the oil.

By testing the most straightforward explanation first, you save time and avoid panic.

How to Apply Occam's Razor

1. Identify the Problem Clearly:

Define exactly what you're trying to explain. The better you understand the question, the easier it is to spot unnecessary assumptions.

2. List All Possible Explanations:

Brainstorm the different ways this problem could have occurred. Don't dismiss any ideas yet.

3. Eliminate Unnecessary Assumptions:

Ask, *What do I need to assume for this explanation to work?* The more assumptions required, the less likely it's true.

4. Start with the Simplest Explanation:

Focus on the explanation with the least assumptions. Test it first. If it works, great! If not, move to the next simplest idea.

Everyday Example of Occam's Razor

Suppose your friend hasn't replied to your text for hours.

- Overthinking: *They're mad at me. They're ghosting me. Maybe I said something wrong.*

- Simplest Explanation: *They're busy or didn't see the message yet.*

Occam's Razor reminds you not to jump to wild conclusions when the truth is much simpler.

Common Pitfalls in Occam's Razor

1. Mistaking Simplicity for Oversimplification:

Just because something sounds simple doesn't mean it's true. Occam's Razor focuses on the *simplest explanation that fits the evidence.* Ignoring evidence leads to flawed reasoning.

2. Ignoring Complex Truths:

Some problems genuinely have complicated causes. If the simplest explanation doesn't hold up, be ready to explore deeper layers.

3. Bias Toward Familiar Ideas:

Simpler doesn't always mean familiar. Occam's Razor helps you find truth, not just what feels comfortable or obvious.

4. Skipping Evidence to Jump to Conclusions:

Occam's Razor isn't about guessing—it's about eliminating unnecessary assumptions. Always test your simplest explanation before accepting it.

Practical Tip: Ask Yourself, "What's the Simplest Path?"

Whenever you're stuck, imagine your problem as a knot. Don't waste time pulling at every thread. Instead, ask: *Where's the easiest place to cut?* This mindset helps you stay focused and efficient, even in chaos.

Takeaway

Occam's Razor isn't just a tool for scientists or philosophers. It's a razor-sharp method for cutting through life's noise. It saves time, energy, and sanity by focusing on what's most likely true.

Before jumping to conclusions, remember: not every mistake is a conspiracy — find out why next.

Chapter 4: Hanlon's Razor

What is Hanlon's Razor?

Hanlon's Razor says: *Never attribute to malice what can be explained by ignorance or carelessness.* In other words, most people aren't plotting against you—they're just not paying attention.

This mental model helps you avoid jumping to negative conclusions. Instead of assuming someone's actions are hostile, consider they might not know better, or they made a mistake. It's about giving others the benefit of the doubt, which leads to better relationships and fewer conflicts.

Why Hanlon's Razor Matters

Blaming others for bad intentions often escalates problems. Miscommunication gets worse. Trust erodes. But if you pause and assume ignorance instead, you're more likely to respond calmly and solve issues effectively.

For example:

- A coworker misses a meeting. Instead of assuming they're lazy or rude, Hanlon's Razor suggests they might have forgotten or mixed up their schedule.

This doesn't excuse bad behavior. But by starting with ignorance, you stay focused on solutions rather than unnecessary blame.

Example: The Unanswered Text

Your friend hasn't replied to your text in hours.

- Malice assumption: *They're ignoring me on purpose.*
- Hanlon's Razor: *They might be busy, distracted, or didn't see it yet.*

This mental model encourages patience and understanding instead of unnecessary frustration.

How to Apply Hanlon's Razor

1. Pause Before Reacting:

When something upsets you, take a moment to consider if it could be a mistake or misunderstanding instead of intentional harm.

2. Ask Questions, Don't Accuse:

Instead of saying, "Why are you doing this to me?" ask, "Did something come up?" or "What happened?" This keeps the conversation productive.

3. Put Yourself in Their Shoes:

Imagine their perspective. Would they have acted this way if they understood the consequences? Ignorance is often more likely than ill intent.

4. Use Evidence, Not Assumptions:

Before concluding that someone acted out of malice, look for proof. Without evidence, ignorance should be your default assumption.

Everyday Example of Hanlon's Razor

Suppose a driver cuts you off in traffic.

- Malice assumption: *They're a reckless jerk who doesn't care about anyone else.*

- Hanlon's Razor: *Maybe they didn't see me, or they're rushing to an emergency.*

This mindset helps you stay calm and avoid unnecessary road rage.

Common Pitfalls in Hanlon's Razor

1. Excusing Genuine Malice:

Some actions are truly harmful or deliberate. Hanlon's Razor is a starting point, not a rule. Once evidence shows intent, act accordingly.

2. Overlooking Patterns:

If someone repeatedly shows carelessness or harmful behavior, it's less likely to be ignorance. Patterns often indicate deeper issues.

3. Failing to Address Problems:

Assuming ignorance doesn't mean ignoring issues. Address mistakes calmly but firmly to prevent future misunderstandings.

Practical Tip: Replace Blame with Curiosity

When someone's actions upset you, start with curiosity instead of anger. Ask yourself, *What could explain this mistake?* This keeps emotions in check and leads to better outcomes.

Takeaway

Hanlon's Razor cuts through emotional overreactions by reminding you to assume ignorance before malice. It encourages understanding, patience, and calmer responses.

But sometimes, thinking in the same direction can cloud your judgment. What if the answer lies in flipping your perspective completely? Let's explore this!

Chapter 5: Inversion

What is Inversion?

Inversion flips your thinking to uncover new insights. Instead of asking, *How do I succeed?* ask, *What would cause me to fail?* Instead of solving a problem directly, think about its opposite.

This mental model works because reversing your perspective often reveals blind spots. By looking at what you *don't* want, you uncover risks and obstacles you might miss otherwise.

Why Inversion Matters

Humans tend to think forward: "How do I achieve X?" Inversion forces you to think backward: "How could I ruin X?" This backward thinking helps identify problems before they arise, making your plans stronger.

Example:

- A business wants to improve customer satisfaction. Using inversion, they ask, *What would make customers unhappy?* Answers like "long wait times" or "poor communication" help them address weaknesses directly.

Example: Planning a Vacation

Normal thinking: *How do I have the best trip?*

Inverted thinking: *What would ruin my trip?*

By focusing on what could go wrong — losing tickets, bad weather, poor planning — you prepare solutions in advance.

How to Apply Inversion

1. Flip the Problem:

Write down the opposite of what you want to achieve. For example, instead of asking, *How do I stay healthy?* ask, *How could I ruin my health?*

2. List Worst-Case Scenarios:

Identify all the ways things could go wrong. This highlights risks you might not have considered.

3. Solve for the Opposite:

Once you know what would cause failure, plan to avoid those pitfalls. This turns potential weaknesses into strengths.

4. Use It to Test Ideas:

When you think you have a good plan, invert it: *What could make this fail?* If you find weaknesses, improve your approach before moving forward.

Everyday Example of Inversion

Imagine you're hosting a dinner party.

Normal thinking: *How do I make the party great?*

Inversion: *What would ruin the party?*

By thinking about potential failures—burnt food, late guests, or running out of drinks—you can plan ahead to prevent them.

Common Pitfalls in Inversion

1. Getting Stuck in Negativity:

Inversion is about identifying risks, not dwelling on problems. Use it to strengthen your plans, not to overthink everything that could go wrong.

2. Ignoring Positive Thinking:

Inversion is a tool, not the whole process. Balance it with forward-thinking strategies to create well-rounded solutions.

3. Overcomplicating Simple Issues:

Not every problem needs inversion. Use it for complex challenges where risks aren't obvious.

Practical Tip: Ask, "What's the Worst That Could Happen?"

For every decision, take a moment to think about the worst-case scenario. Then, plan to avoid it. This habit makes your thinking sharper and your actions smarter.

Takeaway

Inversion flips your thinking to see problems from a fresh angle. It reveals risks, improves plans, and strengthens outcomes.

Next, let's take this clarity even further. What if you could predict your outcomes based on probabilities, not just possibilities?

Chapter 6: Probabilistic Thinking

What is Probabilistic Thinking?

Probabilistic Thinking means understanding that life isn't black and white — it's about probabilities. It's asking: *What are the odds this will happen?* and using that information to make better decisions.

Instead of thinking, *This will definitely work,* you think, *This is 70% likely to work.* It's a way to weigh risks, rewards, and uncertainties so you can act more strategically.

Why Probabilistic Thinking Matters

Decisions based on certainty often fail because life is unpredictable. Probabilistic Thinking prepares you for different outcomes.

For example:

- A gambler bets everything on a risky hand because they feel "lucky" (bad thinking). A probabilistic thinker knows the odds aren't in their favor and folds.

This model doesn't guarantee success, but it makes your odds of winning higher in the long run.

Example: Deciding to Bring an Umbrella

You see a weather forecast showing a 60% chance of rain.

- Binary thinking: *It's either going to rain or it's not. I'll leave the umbrella.*

- Probabilistic Thinking: *There's a 60% chance of rain, so I'll take the umbrella just in case.*

By considering probabilities, you prepare for likely scenarios while staying flexible for surprises.

How to Apply Probabilistic Thinking

1. Think in Percentages:

For every decision, estimate how likely each outcome is. Ask yourself: *What are the odds?*

2. Consider All Possible Outcomes:

Don't just focus on the most likely scenario. Think about what could happen if things go worse or better than expected.

3. Weigh Risks vs. Rewards:

Ask: *Is the reward worth the risk?* If the risk is high and the reward is low, rethink your choice.

4. Improve Your Estimates Over Time:

The more you practice, the better you'll get at predicting outcomes. Use past experiences to refine your understanding of probabilities.

Everyday Example of Probabilistic Thinking

Imagine you're deciding whether to invest in a startup.

- Gut feeling: *This startup is amazing! I'll invest everything.*

- Probabilistic Thinking: *What percentage of startups succeed? If the odds are 10%, I'll invest only what I can afford to lose.*

This approach protects you from big losses while keeping you open to potential rewards.

Common Pitfalls in Probabilistic Thinking

1. Overconfidence in Low-Probability Events:

Just because something is possible doesn't mean it's likely. Avoid fixating on unlikely outcomes.

2. Ignoring Uncertainty:

Probabilistic Thinking doesn't mean you'll predict everything perfectly. It's about managing uncertainty, not eliminating it.

3. Neglecting Rare but High-Impact Events:

While focusing on likely outcomes, don't ignore rare events with big consequences (like natural disasters or major market crashes).

Practical Tip: Use a Probability Scale

When faced with a decision, assign percentages to each possible outcome. Then choose the option with the best balance of high reward and low risk.

Takeaway

Probabilistic Thinking helps you navigate uncertainty with logic and clarity. It's a powerful tool for making smarter decisions in an unpredictable world.

But to take this further, you need to adapt your beliefs when new evidence comes your way. Are you ready to think like a true scientist?

Chapter 7: Bayesian Thinking

What is Bayesian Thinking?

Bayesian Thinking is about adjusting your beliefs as new evidence appears. Instead of clinging to what you *thought* was true, you constantly ask: *What do I know now? How does this change what I believe?*

Named after mathematician Thomas Bayes, this method helps you avoid rigid thinking. It's about being flexible and willing to revise your ideas when the facts change.

Why Bayesian Thinking Matters

Sticking to outdated beliefs is like driving with an old map — it leads you in the wrong direction. Bayesian Thinking ensures you update your "map" with the latest information, improving your decisions over time.

For example:

- You assume someone is rude because they didn't say hello. Later, you learn they didn't see you. Bayesian Thinking adjusts your belief to fit the new evidence.

This model is essential in a fast-changing world, where clinging to old ideas can lead to bad outcomes.

Example: Hiring a New Employee

You interview a candidate who seems perfect on paper. But during the interview, they struggle to answer key questions.

- Fixed Thinking: *Their resume is great, so they'll succeed.*

- Bayesian Thinking: *Their resume looked good, but new evidence (the interview) suggests they might not be the right fit. Let's reevaluate.*

By updating your beliefs with new evidence, you make more informed decisions.

How to Apply Bayesian Thinking

1. Start with a Baseline Belief:

Ask yourself: *What do I currently believe? Why?* Write it down if necessary.

2. Incorporate New Evidence:

When new information becomes available, ask: *Does this support or challenge my belief?*

3. Reassess the Odds:

Adjust your belief based on how strong or weak the new evidence is.

4. Be Willing to Change:

Don't let pride stop you from relooking your beliefs. Flexibility is key.

Everyday Example of Bayesian Thinking

Suppose you assume your favorite restaurant always has great food. But on your last visit, the food was cold.

- Fixed Thinking: *It was just bad luck—I'll keep assuming it's perfect.*

- Bayesian Thinking: *This new evidence lowers the odds that it's always great. I'll try another visit before deciding.*

This approach balances past experience with new information, keeping your beliefs realistic.

Common Pitfalls in Bayesian Thinking

1. Ignoring Strong Evidence:

Don't cling to beliefs if the new evidence clearly contradicts them.

2. Overreacting to Weak Evidence:

Not all new information deserves a big belief change. Consider how reliable and relevant it is.

3. Emotional Bias:

Avoid letting emotions cloud your judgment when evaluating evidence.

Practical Tip: Use "If-Then" Statements

Frame beliefs as conditional: *If X happens, then Y is likely true.* This makes updating your beliefs easier when new evidence arises.

Takeaway

Bayesian Thinking helps you stay open-minded, flexible, and evidence-based. It ensures your beliefs evolve as reality unfolds.

But what happens when the world isn't a single chain of events, but a web of interconnected parts? Let's untangle this complexity next.

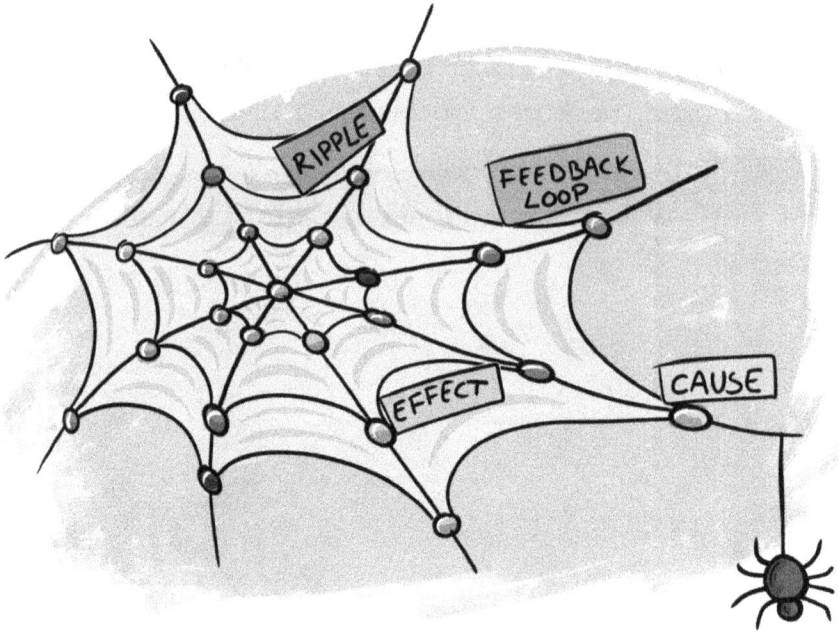

Chapter 8: Systems Thinking

What is Systems Thinking?

Systems Thinking means looking at the big picture. Instead of focusing on one part of a problem, you see how all the parts connect. It's about understanding that life works like a web.

This model helps you think beyond simple cause-and-effect. Instead, you recognize that problems and solutions are often part of larger, interconnected systems.

Why Systems Thinking Matters

When people focus too narrowly, they miss how changes in one area affect everything else.

For example:

- A company cuts costs by reducing customer support staff (short-term fix). Customers get frustrated, leave bad reviews, and sales drop (long-term ripple effect).

Systems Thinking prevents short-sighted decisions by helping you see how actions impact the whole system.

Example: Fixing Traffic

Imagine a city adds more lanes to reduce traffic congestion.

- Linear Thinking: *More lanes = less traffic.*

- Systems Thinking: *More lanes might encourage more drivers, worsening traffic over time.*

By considering the system as a whole, you uncover unintended consequences and make smarter decisions.

How to Apply Systems Thinking

1. Map the System:

Identify all the parts of the problem and how they connect. Use tools like flowcharts or diagrams to visualize the system.

2. Think in Feedback Loops:

Ask: *What happens next? And then?* Look for positive loops (which amplify change) and negative loops (which stabilize the system).

3. Zoom Out:

Don't focus on one piece of the puzzle. Ask: *How does this fit into the bigger picture?*

4. Consider Long-Term Effects:

Look beyond immediate results. Ask: *What are the second- and third-order effects of this decision?*

Everyday Example of Systems Thinking

Imagine you're trying to save money by eating out less.

- Linear Thinking: *Spend less on restaurants = save money.*

- Systems Thinking: *Eating out less saves money, but will I spend more on groceries? Will I miss social connections that restaurants provide? How will this affect my time and energy?*

Systems Thinking helps you plan solutions that balance all factors, not just one.

Common Pitfalls in Systems Thinking

1. Overcomplicating the System:

Not every problem requires mapping every connection. Focus on the most important parts of the system.

2. Ignoring Delays:

Some effects take time to appear. Don't assume immediate results mean the system is working perfectly.

3. Fixating on Single Solutions:

Systems often need multiple adjustments, not one magic fix.

4. Underestimating Human Behavior:

Systems involve people, who may act unpredictably. Include emotional and social factors in your analysis.

Practical Tip: Ask, "What Happens Next?"

For any decision, imagine pulling a thread in a web. Think about the immediate effects, the ripple effects, and the feedback loops.

Takeaway

Systems Thinking helps you navigate complexity by seeing the whole picture, not just isolated parts. It makes your decisions smarter, more balanced, and better for the long term.

But to truly harness this, you need to understand one of nature's most powerful forces—compounding. Let's explore this further.

Chapter 9: Compound Interest

What is Compound Interest?

Compound Interest is the idea that growth builds on itself over time. It's not just about earning rewards—it's about earning rewards on those rewards.

This concept is most often used in finance (like saving money), but it applies to everything: learning, habits, relationships, and skills. Small, consistent actions lead to exponential results when given enough time.

Why Compound Interest Matters

Humans tend to focus on immediate results, but real progress happens slowly at first, then explodes.

For example:

- Investing $1,000 at 5% interest earns $50 in the first year. In the second year, you earn interest not just on $1,000 but on $1,050. Over decades, this snowballs into massive growth.

The same happens in life: small daily improvements lead to extraordinary results over time.

Example: Learning a Skill

Imagine you practice the guitar for 20 minutes a day.

- Short-term thinking: *I don't see much improvement after a week.*

- Compound Interest: *In a year, I'll have practiced over 120 hours. Each session builds on the last, creating exponential growth.*

This approach helps you stay patient and consistent, knowing the results will come.

How to Apply Compound Interest

1. Start Small but Consistent:

Focus on small, repeatable actions. Even a little effort compounds over time.

2. Be Patient:

Compound growth is slow at first. Stick with it, even if results aren't immediately visible.

3. Focus on High-Impact Areas:

Apply compounding to things that matter most, like skills, relationships, or finances.

4. Avoid Negative Compounding:

Bad habits compound, too. Smoking, procrastination, or debt grow into bigger problems over time. Stop them early.

Everyday Example of Compound Interest

Suppose you want to get fit.

- Short-term thinking: One workout won't make a difference.

- Compound Interest: Daily exercise, even for 15 minutes, will add up to better health and energy over time.

The same principle applies to learning, saving, or building good habits.

Common Pitfalls in Compound Interest

1. Impatience:

Many people quit before compounding kicks in. Remember, the biggest growth happens later.

2. Inconsistent Effort:

Skipping small actions disrupts the compounding effect. Stay consistent.

3. Underestimating Long-Term Impact:

Small habits—good or bad—have huge consequences over time. Choose wisely.

Practical Tip: Think in Decades

Ask yourself: *If I repeat this action daily for 10 years, what will the result be?* This helps you focus on actions that truly matter.

Takeaway

Compound Interest shows that small, consistent efforts lead to massive rewards over time. It's a powerful reminder to focus on the long game.

Next, let's narrow our focus. What if success comes not from knowing *everything,* but from mastering what you know *best?*

Chapter 10: Circle of Competence

What is the Circle of Competence?

The Circle of Competence is the idea that you perform best when you stick to what you know well. It's about understanding your strengths and weaknesses and focusing on areas where you have the most expertise.

This mental model reminds you to avoid overconfidence in unfamiliar areas. It's fine to step outside your comfort zone, but true success often comes from operating where you're skilled and knowledgeable.

Why the Circle of Competence Matters

When you stray too far outside your expertise, mistakes happen.

For example:

- A chef might think they can run a restaurant just because they can cook. But without knowledge of business management, they could struggle.

- A friend gives you stock tips, but you don't understand the market. Investing without knowledge could lead to big losses.

Knowing what's *inside* your Circle of Competence keeps you focused and prevents costly errors.

Example: Picking Investments

Imagine you're deciding between investing in real estate or tech startups.

- Outside the Circle: *I don't understand how tech startups work, but I'll take a guess.*

- Inside the Circle: *I know real estate well and can make informed decisions.*

Sticking to what you know reduces risk and boosts confidence in your choices.

How to Apply the Circle of Competence

1. Define Your Strengths:

Ask: *What am I truly knowledgeable about? Where do I have experience or proven success?* Write it down to clarify your focus.

2. Acknowledge Weaknesses:

Be honest about what's outside your expertise. Recognizing limits isn't a failure—it's wisdom.

3. Learn Strategically:

If you want to expand your circle, do so intentionally. Study, practice, and build experience in new areas before making decisions there.

4. Seek Help Outside Your Circle:

When faced with something unfamiliar, rely on experts. You don't need to master everything—sometimes the smartest move is to ask for advice.

Everyday Example of the Circle of Competence

Suppose your sink is leaking.

- Outside the Circle: *I'll try to fix it myself even though I know nothing about plumbing.*

- Inside the Circle: *I'll call a plumber because that's their area of expertise, not mine.*

Knowing your limits saves time, money, and unnecessary stress.

Common Pitfalls in the Circle of Competence

1. Overestimating Your Knowledge:

Confidence is good, but overconfidence leads to mistakes. Stay humble about what you know.

2. Never Expanding the Circle:

While staying inside your circle is wise, don't fear learning new skills. Expanding your competence thoughtfully is how you grow.

3. Ignoring Expert Advice:

Thinking you can figure everything out yourself often leads to errors. Rely on others when needed.

4. Confusing Familiarity with Expertise:

Just because you're familiar with something doesn't mean you're competent at it. For example, using social media doesn't make you a marketing expert.

Practical Tip: Ask, "Am I Qualified to Decide?"

Before making a big decision, pause and ask: *Do I truly understand this? Am I the best person to handle it?* If not, it's time to step back or seek help.

Takeaway

The Circle of Competence keeps you grounded, helping you play to your strengths while avoiding unnecessary risks. It's not about staying small—it's about making thoughtful, informed choices.

Success starts with knowing your limits and using that knowledge wisely. Let's unpack this further.

Learning and Adaptability Models

Chapter 11: The Learning Curve

What is the Learning Curve?

The Learning Curve shows how people improve with practice. At first, progress is slow and frustrating because everything feels unfamiliar. Over time, things "click," and growth speeds up. Eventually, improvement slows again as you approach mastery.

This mental model reminds you that learning is a process. You won't become great overnight, but steady effort leads to results.

Why the Learning Curve Matters

Understanding the Learning Curve keeps you motivated when things feel tough at first. Many people quit early because they don't see progress. Knowing that improvement takes time helps you push through the hard part.

For example:

- A new job might feel overwhelming at first, but every day you learn a little more.

- Learning to play the piano may seem impossible at first, but practice builds skill until it becomes second nature.

The Learning Curve is a reminder that perseverance pays off.

Example: Starting a New Workout Routine

At first, the exercises feel awkward, and progress seems slow. After a few weeks, movements feel easier, and you notice real improvement. The steep part of the curve has passed, and now you're steadily growing.

How to Apply the Learning Curve

1. Expect Struggle at First:

Remind yourself that the beginning is the hardest part. Growth will come with time and effort.

2. Set Small Goals:

Focus on manageable steps to stay motivated. Each small win moves you along the curve.

3. Be Consistent:

Regular practice is the key to climbing the curve. Even small amounts of effort add up over time.

4. Recognize Plateaus:

When improvement slows, it doesn't mean you've stopped learning. Mastery takes patience, so keep going.

Everyday Example of the Learning Curve

Imagine you're learning to cook.

- Day 1: You burn the pasta and forget the salt.

- Day 30: You're confidently making sauces from scratch.

The Learning Curve shows that every awkward mistake brings you closer to skill.

Common Pitfalls in the Learning Curve

1. Quitting Too Soon:

Many people give up during the hardest phase, missing out on growth just around the corner.

2. Comparing Yourself to Others:

Everyone's curve is different. Comparing your progress to others can lead to frustration. Focus on your own growth.

3. Overestimating Early Progress:

Rapid improvement at first can create unrealistic expectations for long-term growth. Be patient.

4. Ignoring the Role of Feedback:

To climb the curve effectively, use feedback to correct mistakes and improve faster.

Practical Tip: Track Your Progress

Keep a journal or log to track small improvements. Looking back at where you started is a great motivator when the journey feels slow.

Takeaway

The Learning Curve reminds you that growth is slow at first but accelerates with practice. It's a powerful motivator to stay consistent and patient, even when progress feels invisible.

Mastery isn't about speed; it's about persistence. Let's explore how feedback can amplify your progress.

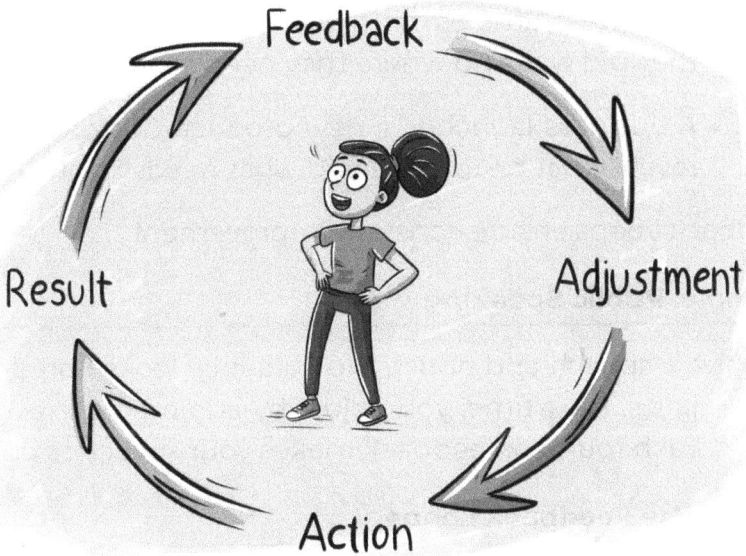

Chapter 12: Feedback Loops

What are Feedback Loops?

Feedback Loops are cycles of action, feedback, and adjustment. You try something, see the results, and use that information to improve your next attempt.

Feedback Loops are how we learn and adapt. The more you listen to feedback, the better you become.

Why Feedback Loops Matter

Without feedback, progress is random. Feedback Loops provide the information needed to refine your actions and get better results.

For example:

- A student studies for a test. Their grade shows what they did well and where they need more work.

- A business launches a new product. Customer reviews reveal what people like and what needs improvement.

Feedback Loops ensure constant improvement.

Example: Public Speaking

You give a speech and notice the audience looks bored during certain parts. Next time, you adjust by adding more engaging stories. Each round of feedback makes your speeches better.

How to Use Feedback Loops

1. Act and Observe:

Try something and pay attention to the results. What worked? What didn't?

2. Seek Honest Feedback:

Ask for input from people you trust. Constructive criticism is more valuable than vague praise.

3. Make Small Adjustments:

Use feedback to tweak your approach. Don't overhaul everything at once—small changes work best.

4. Repeat the Cycle:

Improvement is ongoing. Keep using the loop to refine your skills over time.

Everyday Example of Feedback Loops

Imagine you're learning to bake bread.

- First loaf: It's too dense.

- Feedback: The dough didn't rise long enough.

- Adjustment: Next time, you let it rise longer.

Each loaf gets better as you refine your process.

Common Pitfalls in Feedback Loops

1. Ignoring Feedback:

Without listening to feedback, you can't improve. Be open to constructive criticism.

2. Taking Feedback Personally:

Feedback is about your actions, not your worth. Use it as a tool for growth.

3. Changing Too Much at Once:

Overhauling everything makes it hard to tell what worked. Adjust one thing at a time.

4. Seeking Only Positive Feedback:

Honest criticism is more useful than empty praise. Surround yourself with people who tell you the truth.

Practical Tip: Ask, "What Can I Do Better?"

After every effort, ask yourself or others: *What worked? What didn't? What can I improve next time?* This keeps the loop moving.

Takeaway

Feedback Loops are the engine of improvement. By acting, listening, and adjusting, you can achieve steady progress in any area of life.

Growth isn't about perfection — it's about refinement. Let's discuss how to make learning even more effective.

Chapter 13: Meta-Learning

What is Meta-Learning?

Meta-Learning means learning *how to learn.* Instead of focusing only on what to study, you focus on the process of learning itself. It's about discovering the techniques, strategies, and habits that make you a more efficient learner.

This mental model is like having a blueprint for your brain. When you understand how learning works, you can tackle any subject faster and better.

Why Meta-Learning Matters

People often waste time using ineffective learning methods.

For example:

- Cramming for a test might work short-term but fails in the long run.

- Reading a textbook passively is slower and less effective than active engagement, like testing yourself.

Meta-Learning saves time and effort by teaching you *how* to learn smarter, not harder.

Example: Learning a Language

Instead of memorizing hundreds of vocabulary words in isolation, you focus on conversation practice and real-life contexts. By learning how to learn languages effectively, you progress faster and retain more.

How to Practice Meta-Learning

1. Understand Your Learning Style:

Do you learn best through visuals, hands-on practice, or listening? Tailor your methods to what works for you.

2. Use Proven Techniques:

Strategies like spaced repetition (reviewing over time), active recall (testing yourself), and chunking (breaking material into small pieces) boost retention.

3. Focus on Key Principles First:

Learn the most important concepts before diving into details. Understanding the foundation helps everything else make sense.

4. Reflect on What Works:

After every learning session, ask: *What helped me learn? What didn't?* Adjust your approach for next time.

Everyday Example of Meta-Learning

Imagine you're learning to cook. Instead of jumping into advanced recipes, you first learn the basics of seasoning, knife skills, and cooking techniques. These fundamentals make every recipe easier to master.

Common Pitfalls in Meta-Learning

1. Ignoring the Process:

Focusing only on the material, not the method, can slow progress. Meta-Learning keeps your process efficient.

2. Not Adapting to the Subject:

Different topics require different strategies. Learning math might need problem-solving practice, while learning music requires repetition and feedback.

3. Overloading Yourself:

Trying to learn everything at once is overwhelming. Focus on mastering one thing at a time.

4. Skipping Self-Reflection:

Without reflecting on your learning process, you miss opportunities to improve.

Practical Tip: Keep a Learning Journal

Track what methods you used, what worked well, and what didn't. Over time, this journal becomes your personal guide to learning effectively.

Takeaway

Meta-Learning is the ultimate skill. By mastering how to learn, you unlock faster, smarter growth in every area of life.

It's not about learning everything — it's about learning efficiently. Let's learn more about how small, steady progress can amplify this further.

Chapter 14: Incremental Growth

What is Incremental Growth?

Incremental Growth is the idea that small, consistent improvements add up to big results over time. Instead of trying to change everything at once, you focus on getting just a little better each day.

This mental model is about steady progress, not perfection.

Why Incremental Growth Matters

Big, dramatic changes often fail because they're overwhelming. Incremental Growth works because it's manageable.

For example:

- Instead of trying to lose 20 pounds in a month, you aim to lose 1 pound a week.

- Instead of writing a novel in a week, you write one page a day.

These small wins build momentum and keep you motivated.

Example: Learning to Run

You want to run a marathon, but you've never run before.

- Big Leap Thinking: Try to run 10 miles on day one, fail, and feel discouraged.

- Incremental Growth: Start with a 1-mile jog. Add a little more distance each week. Eventually, you build the stamina to finish the race.

How to Apply Incremental Growth

1. Set Small Goals:

Break big goals into tiny, achievable steps. Focus on what you can improve today.

2. Track Progress:

Keep a journal or chart to see how far you've come. Small wins build motivation.

3. Focus on Consistency:

Daily effort matters more than big, irregular bursts. Build habits that stick.

4. Celebrate Milestones:

Acknowledge progress along the way. Small rewards keep you motivated.

Everyday Example of Incremental Growth

Suppose you're learning to draw.

- Day 1: You sketch basic shapes.

- Day 30: You're adding shading and detail.

- Day 365: You're creating full, detailed drawings.

Each day's small practice adds up to big improvement over time.

Common Pitfalls in Incremental Growth

1. Expecting Instant Results:

Growth takes time. Don't get discouraged if progress feels slow.

2. Skipping Steps:

Jumping ahead too soon often leads to mistakes. Focus on mastering each step.

3. Losing Consistency:

Sporadic effort disrupts momentum. Stick to regular practice.

4. Underestimating Small Wins:

Tiny improvements might seem insignificant, but they create lasting change.

Practical Tip: Ask, "What's My 1% Today?"

Each day, focus on improving by just 1%. Over time, these small gains lead up to big transformations.

Takeaway

Incremental Growth shows that small, steady effort is the key to achieving big goals. It's not about perfection—it's about persistence.

Progress starts with a single step, and each step brings you closer to mastery. Let's reflect on how mindset plays a role in approaching new challenges.

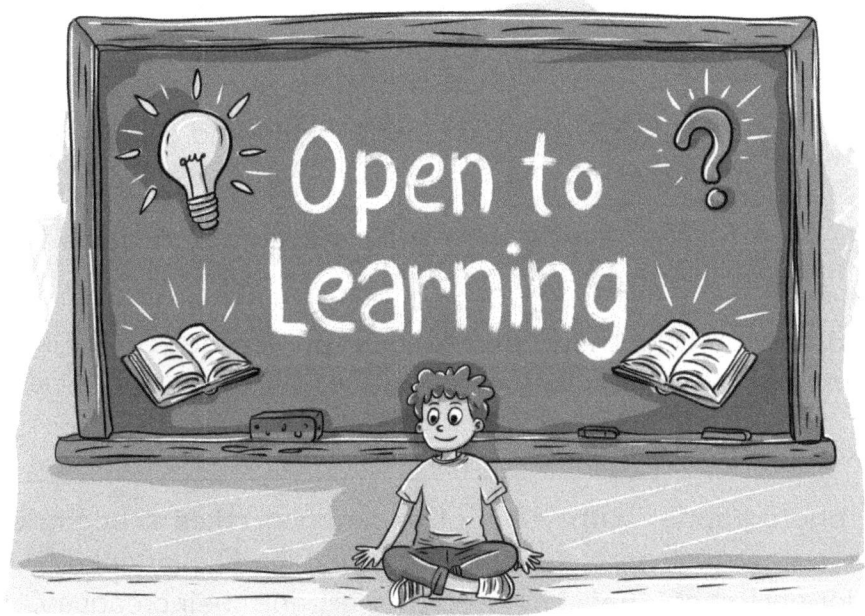

Chapter 15: Shoshin (Beginner's Mind)

What is Shoshin (Beginner's Mind)?

Shoshin is a Zen concept that means approaching every topic with the curiosity of a beginner. Even if you're experienced, you stay open to learning new things.

This mindset helps you avoid the trap of thinking you already "know it all." It encourages curiosity, humility, and a willingness to see things in fresh ways.

Why Shoshin Matters

Experts often stop growing because they think they've already mastered a topic. Beginners, on the other hand, are full of curiosity. Shoshin keeps that spark alive, no matter how much experience you have.

For example:

- A chef revisits the basics of cooking and discovers new techniques.

- A teacher learns from their students and gains fresh perspectives.

Shoshin unlocks new possibilities by letting go of rigid thinking.

Example: Revisiting a Skill

A photographer with years of experience takes a beginner's course and learns techniques they had overlooked. By adopting a beginner's mindset, they expand their creativity.

How to Practice Shoshin

1. Ask Questions:

Approach every topic with curiosity. Even simple questions can lead to amazing insights.

2. Challenge Assumptions:

Ask yourself: *What do I think I know? Could I be missing something?* Stay open to new ideas.

3. Learn from Everyone:

Beginners often notice things that experts miss. Be willing to learn from people with less experience.

4. Stay Humble:

Recognize that there's always more to learn. No one knows everything.

Everyday Example of Shoshin

Imagine you're reading a book about a topic you already know well.

- Without Shoshin: You skim through, assuming there's nothing new.

- With Shoshin: You read carefully and discover fresh insights.

Staying curious helps you grow, even in areas where you're skilled.

Common Pitfalls in Shoshin

1. Clinging to Expertise:

Thinking you're an expert can block you from seeing new perspectives.

2. Ignoring Simple Ideas:

Complex problems often have simple solutions. Don't dismiss basic ideas as "too obvious."

3. Assuming Growth Stops:

Mastery is never final. There's always room to improve and adapt.

4. Fearing Failure:

Beginners often make mistakes. Embrace them as part of the learning process.

Practical Tip: Say, "What Can I Learn Today?"

Before tackling any task, ask yourself this question. It sets the tone for curiosity and openness.

Takeaway

Shoshin reminds you to stay curious and open. Growth happens when you approach life with fresh eyes and a beginner's curiosity.

Mastery begins with an open mind, but success often depends on how quickly you adapt to new challenges.

Chapter 16: Agility in Learning

What is Agility in Learning?

Agility in Learning means adapting quickly when faced with new challenges or information. It's the ability to adjust your approach, pick up new skills, and thrive in unpredictable situations.

This mindset is essential in a fast-changing world where yesterday's knowledge might not solve tomorrow's problems.

Why Agility in Learning Matters

Non-flexible thinking limits your ability to succeed when things change. Agility keeps creative, and ready for anything.

For example:

- A business owner adapts to a new trend by learning online marketing.

- A student switches study methods after realizing their old approach isn't effective.

The faster you adapt, the faster you grow.

Example: Adapting to Remote Work

When offices switch to remote work, an agile learner quickly masters video conferencing and digital tools. Instead of resisting change, they embrace it and excel.

How to Develop Agility in Learning

1. Stay Curious:

Treat every challenge as an opportunity to learn. Ask: *What can this teach me?*

2. Experiment Often:

Try new methods, tools, or ideas. Don't fear failure—it's how you learn what works.

3. Be Open to Feedback:

Listen to others and use their input to adjust your approach.

4. Let Go of Old Habits:

If something isn't working, don't cling to it. Be willing to change course.

Everyday Example of Agility in Learning

Suppose your phone's operating system changes.

- Fixed Thinking: *This update is confusing. I'll ignore it.*

- Agile Thinking: *I'll take 10 minutes to explore the new features and learn how they work.*

Adapting quickly makes you more efficient and confident.

Common Pitfalls in Agility

1. Resisting Change:

Fear of the unknown can hold you back. Embrace change as a chance to grow.

2. Overthinking Adjustments:

Agility doesn't mean perfection. Focus on progress, not flawless execution.

3. Clinging to Comfort Zones:

Growth happens outside your comfort zone. Push yourself to try new things.

4. Ignoring Long-Term Impact:

Agility is about quick changes, but keep the big picture in mind.

Practical Tip: Ask, "What's My Next Move?"

When faced with a challenge, focus on your next step. Don't get stuck overanalyzing—act and adjust as you go.

Takeaway

Agility in Learning helps you adapt and thrive in a world of constant change. The faster you adjust, the more opportunities you can seize.

Growth thrives on flexibility, but true mastery requires sharpening your mindset. Let's unpack this further.

This isn't how I've always done it – I don't think it'll work

But what if trying something new gets better results?

Chapter 17: Mental Flexibility

What is Mental Flexibility?

Mental Flexibility is the ability to adapt your thinking when faced with new ideas, unexpected changes, or challenges. It's the opposite of rigid thinking—it means being open to reexamining your beliefs and approaches without clinging to what's familiar.

This mindset helps you think creatively, solve problems, and thrive in uncertain situations.

Why Mental Flexibility Matters

Stubborn thinking limits progress. Mental Flexibility allows you to shift strategies, find better solutions, and navigate life's twists and turns.

For example:

- A manager reworks their team's goals when market trends shift.
- A student changes their study methods after realizing their old approach isn't effective.

Mental Flexibility lets you grow instead of staying stuck.

Example: A New Perspective on a Problem

You're struggling to assemble a piece of furniture. Instead of forcing the same method, you reread the instructions and find a simpler solution.

How to Build Mental Flexibility

1. Question Your Assumptions:

Ask yourself: *What if I'm wrong? Is there another way to see this?*

2. Seek Diverse Opinions:

Talk to people with different perspectives. Their insights can help you see beyond your usual thinking.

3. Practice "What If" Scenarios:

Imagine alternate outcomes or solutions to problems. This stretches your thinking.

4. Embrace Mistakes:

Mistakes show where old methods aren't working. Use them as opportunities to adjust and grow.

Everyday Example of Mental Flexibility

Suppose a recipe isn't working because you're missing an ingredient.

- Rigid Thinking: *I can't make this dish without that ingredient.*

- Flexible Thinking: *What can I substitute to make it work?*

This approach turns obstacles into opportunities.

Common Pitfalls in Mental Flexibility

1. Clinging to Comfort:

Staying with familiar ideas feels safe but limits growth. Push yourself to explore new options.

2. Overthinking Adjustments:

Don't paralyze yourself with too many possibilities. Test a solution and adapt as needed.

3. Confusing Flexibility with Indecision:

Flexibility means adapting, not endlessly questioning every choice. Stay focused.

4. Ignoring Emotional Barriers:

Sometimes, stubbornness comes from fear or pride. Recognize these emotions and work through them.

Practical Tip: Practice "Yes, And..." Thinking

When brainstorming or problem-solving, build on ideas instead of shutting them down. Say, *Yes, and what if we also...?* This encourages open, flexible thinking.

Takeaway

Mental Flexibility helps you adapt, innovate, and grow by shifting your mindset when circumstances demand it. Mastering it ensures you're always ready for life's surprises.

Now, let's reflect on the past to prepare for the future.

Chapter 18: Self-Reflection

What is Self-Reflection?

Self-Reflection is the practice of looking back on your actions, decisions, and experiences to learn from them. It's about asking: *What did I do well? What could I improve?*

This mental model helps you understand yourself better, so you can make smarter choices moving forward.

Why Self-Reflection Matters

Without reflection, you risk repeating the same mistakes or missing opportunities to improve. Self-Reflection turns experience into wisdom.

For example:

- An athlete reviews their performance after a game to identify strengths and areas for growth.

- A professional evaluates their week to see what tasks were most productive.

Reflection sharpens your judgment and boosts your progress.

Example: Reviewing a Job Interview

After a job interview, you think about what went well and what you could improve for next time. This helps you prepare better answers and build confidence.

How to Practice Self-Reflection

1. Schedule Time for Reflection:

Set aside a few minutes daily or weekly to review your actions and decisions.

2. Ask Specific Questions:

Reflect on key moments by asking: *What worked? What didn't? What will I do differently?*

3. Write It Down:

Keeping a journal helps organize your thoughts and track patterns over time.

4. Focus on Solutions, Not Regrets:

Use reflection to grow, not to dwell on mistakes. Focus on what you can learn and improve.

Everyday Example of Self-Reflection

Imagine you've just hosted a party.

- Reflect: Did the guests have fun? Did I prepare enough food? How can I make the next one better?

This process helps you improve with every experience.

Common Pitfalls in Self-Reflection

1. Overthinking Past Actions:

Reflect, but don't get stuck dwelling on mistakes. Use the past to improve the future.

2. Focusing Only on Negatives:

Celebrate your successes, too. Reflection should include what you did well.

3. Skipping the "Next Steps":

Reflection is useless without action. Always ask: *What will I do differently next time?*

4. Judging Yourself Harshly:

Be honest but kind to yourself. Reflection is about growth, not self-criticism.

Practical Tip: Use the "Three W's"

When reflecting, ask: *What went well? What didn't? What will I do next time?* This keeps your reflection focused and actionable.

Takeaway

Self-Reflection turns experience into growth by helping you analyze the past and improve for the future.

Mistakes are part of growth — let's explore how to embrace them as opportunities for learning.

FAILURES ARE OPPORTUNITIES TO REBUILD STRONGER.

Chapter 19: Failure Analysis

What is Failure Analysis?

Failure Analysis is the process of breaking down mistakes to understand what went wrong and why. It's about learning from failures instead of fearing or ignoring them.

Failures aren't the end — they're stepping stones to success if you analyze them thoughtfully.

Why Failure Analysis Matters

Many people avoid thinking about failure because it feels uncomfortable. But without analyzing mistakes, you miss valuable lessons.

For example:

- A failed project teaches you what to avoid next time.

- A lost game helps you identify weaknesses to improve your strategy.

Failures are valuable teachers when you pay attention.

Example: A Missed Deadline

You miss an important deadline. By analyzing the failure, you realize poor time management was the cause. Next time, you set reminders and break tasks into smaller steps.

How to Perform Failure Analysis

1. Identify the Failure:

Be specific about what went wrong. Avoid vague statements like "I messed up."

2. Find the Root Cause:

Ask, *Why did this happen?* Dig deep to uncover the underlying reasons.

3. Extract Lessons:

Focus on what the failure taught you. What can you do differently next time?

4. Take Action:

Use the insights to make a clear plan for improvement.

Everyday Example of Failure Analysis

Imagine your first attempt at baking a cake fails because it's undercooked.

- Analysis: *Why did this happen? I didn't preheat the oven properly.*

- Lesson: *Next time, I'll double-check the temperature before starting.*

By analyzing the mistake, you improve your chances of success.

Common Pitfalls in Failure Analysis

1. Blaming Others:

Focus on what you can control instead of shifting blame.

2. Dwelling on the Failure:

Learn from it, then move on. Don't let one mistake define you.

3. Ignoring Patterns:

If similar failures happen repeatedly, look for patterns and address the root cause.

4. Avoiding the Process:

Avoiding failure analysis prevents growth. Embrace it as a learning tool.

Practical Tip: Write a "Failure Postmortem"

After a failure, write down what happened, why it happened, and what you'll do differently. This turns the experience into a learning moment.

Takeaway

Failure Analysis transforms mistakes into opportunities for growth. Every failure contains a lesson — your job is to find it and use it wisely.

True growth comes when you challenge what you already believe—let's discuss this further.

Chapter 20: Challenge Bias

What is Challenge Bias?

Challenge Bias is the habit of actively seeking evidence that contradicts your beliefs. It's the opposite of Confirmation Bias, which makes people focus only on information that supports what they already think.

This mental model forces you to confront blind spots and refine your thinking by exposing it to scrutiny.

Why Challenge Bias Matters

When you avoid challenging your beliefs, you risk holding onto flawed ideas. This can lead to poor decisions and missed opportunities.

For example:

- A scientist tests a hypothesis by trying to disprove it, ensuring their conclusions are strong.

- A manager questions their strategy by seeking input from skeptics, leading to better decisions.

Challenging bias helps you avoid echo chambers and strengthens your understanding.

Example: Choosing a Career Path

Suppose you're convinced you want to be a lawyer. By challenging your bias, you shadow a lawyer for a week and realize the work doesn't align with your passions. This saves you years of pursuing the wrong goal.

How to Challenge Bias

1. Seek Contradictory Evidence:

Actively look for information that opposes your views. Ask, *What would prove me wrong?*

2. Listen to Opposing Opinions:

Talk to people who disagree with you. Their perspective might reveal blind spots.

3. Play Devil's Advocate:

Argue against your own beliefs. This tests the strength of your ideas.

4. Ask "What If" Questions:

Explore scenarios where your assumptions might not hold true.

Everyday Example of Challenging Bias

Imagine you believe a certain diet is the healthiest.

- Without Challenging Bias: You only read articles supporting the diet.

- With Challenging Bias: You research critiques of the diet and consult nutrition experts.

This approach helps you make a more informed decision.

Common Pitfalls in Challenging Bias

1. Avoiding Discomfort:

Confronting opposing views can feel uncomfortable, but it's essential for growth.

2. Dismissing Contradictory Evidence:

Don't ignore valid criticism just because it challenges your beliefs.

3. Becoming Defensive:

Focus on understanding, not winning arguments.

4. Falling into Cynicism:

Challenging bias doesn't mean doubting everything—it's about questioning thoughtfully.

Practical Tip: Ask, "What Would Prove Me Wrong?"

For any belief, imagine the evidence that could change your mind. This keeps your thinking balanced and open.

Takeaway

Challenging Bias helps you grow by exposing flaws in your thinking. By questioning your beliefs, you refine your understanding and make smarter decisions.

True wisdom comes from seeing the full picture, even if it means questioning yourself. Let's explore decision-making tools that turn insight into action.

Decision-Making Models

Chapter 21: Cost-Benefit Analysis

What is Cost-Benefit Analysis?

Cost-Benefit Analysis weighs the benefits of a decision against its costs. It helps you determine whether something is worth doing by comparing the value you'll gain to what you'll lose.

This model ensures your choices are rational and focused on maximizing value.

Why Cost-Benefit Analysis Matters

Without evaluating costs and benefits, you risk overcommitting to poor decisions. Cost-Benefit Analysis helps you allocate time, money, and energy wisely.

For example:

- A company decides whether to launch a new product by analyzing potential profits versus development costs.

- A student weighs the benefits of studying late against the cost of losing sleep.

This tool simplifies complex decisions by focusing on what matters most.

Example: Buying a New Car

You're considering upgrading your car.

- Benefits: Reliability, fuel efficiency, comfort.

- Costs: Purchase price, insurance, maintenance.

If the benefits outweigh the costs for your budget, the decision makes sense. If not, it's better to wait.

How to Perform a Cost-Benefit Analysis

1. List All Costs:

Include money, time, effort, and opportunity costs (what you're giving up).

2. List All Benefits:

Think about tangible and intangible gains, like happiness, convenience, or savings.

3. Quantify Where Possible:

Assign numbers or values to each factor to make comparisons easier.

4. Compare and Decide:

If the benefits outweigh the costs significantly, it's a good choice. If not, reconsider.

Everyday Example of Cost-Benefit Analysis

Imagine deciding whether to take an evening class.

- Costs: Tuition, time away from family, effort to study.

- Benefits: New skills, career advancement, personal growth.

Weighing these factors helps you make an informed decision.

Common Pitfalls in Cost-Benefit Analysis

1. Ignoring Intangible Costs or Benefits:

Not everything is easily measured. Consider emotional or social factors, too.

2. Overcomplicating the Process:

Focus on the most important costs and benefits. Avoid getting lost in minor details.

3. Bias Toward Immediate Rewards:

Short-term benefits can blind you to long-term costs. Stay objective.

4. Underestimating Indirect Costs:

Think about ripple effects. For example, a new hobby might cost more time than expected.

Practical Tip: Use a Simple Chart

Create a two-column list with "Costs" on one side and "Benefits" on the other. This visual tool makes comparisons clearer.

Takeaway

Cost-Benefit Analysis simplifies decisions by focusing on value. It ensures your choices are logical, not emotional.

Making decisions is about balancing what you have and what you gain. Let's continue refining your decision-making skills.

Chapter 22: Expected Value

What is Expected Value?

Expected Value (EV) is a way to predict the average outcome of a decision by combining probabilities and rewards. Instead of guessing, you ask: *What's the most logical choice based on the potential payoff and its likelihood?*

This model is essential for making decisions under uncertainty, whether in business, finance, or daily life.

Why Expected Value Matters

Gut feelings often lead to poor decisions because they ignore probabilities. Expected Value forces you to think logically, weighing risks and rewards.

For example:

- A gambler might bet on a long shot with a big payout but low EV.

- A business might invest in a product that has a smaller payout but higher EV because it's more likely to succeed.

Thinking in EV helps you avoid costly mistakes.

Example: Choosing a Lottery Ticket

You're considering buying a lottery ticket for $5. The jackpot is $1 million, but the odds are 1 in 10 million.

- EV = ($1,000,000 × 1/10,000,000) - $5 = -$4.90.

The negative EV shows that buying the ticket isn't logical — it's a losing bet on average.

How to Use Expected Value

1. List Potential Outcomes:

Identify all possible results of your decision.

2. Assign Probabilities:

Estimate how likely each outcome is. Use research or experience to guide you.

3. Calculate Payoffs:

Multiply each outcome's probability by its reward or cost.

4. Sum the Results:

Add up all the values. A positive EV suggests the decision is worth pursuing.

Everyday Example of Expected Value

Imagine deciding whether to leave early for work.

- Staying later saves time, but there's a 50% chance of hitting traffic, costing 30 minutes.

- Leaving earlier avoids traffic, saving 20 minutes.

Calculate the EV for each option to make the best choice.

Common Pitfalls in Expected Value

1. Overestimating Probabilities:

Be realistic about the likelihood of outcomes. Wishful thinking skews EV.

2. Ignoring Emotional Factors:

EV focuses on logic but doesn't account for stress, happiness, or other intangibles.

3. Failing to Reassess:

As new information arises, update your probabilities and EV calculations.

4. Underestimating Rare, High-Impact Events:

Include scenarios with low probability but significant consequences.

Practical Tip: Use the EV Formula

For any decision, apply the formula:

$$EV = (Probability × Reward) - Cost.$$

Takeaway

Expected Value sharpens your ability to evaluate uncertain decisions logically. It balances risks and rewards, helping you choose wisely.

With this tool, let's examine what happens when opportunities come with hidden trade-offs.

Chapter 23: Opportunity Cost

What is Opportunity Cost?

Opportunity Cost is the value of what you give up when making a choice. Every decision means saying no to something else. This model helps you weigh not just the benefits of what you choose but also the costs of what you leave behind.

Why Opportunity Cost Matters

Focusing only on what you gain blinds you to hidden trade-offs. Opportunity Cost makes you think critically about whether your choice is truly the best one.

For example:

- Spending $50 on a dinner out means you can't spend that money on savings or another activity.

- Choosing a high-paying job might mean sacrificing time with family.

Every choice has a cost—it's up to you to evaluate it.

Example: Starting a Business

You invest $10,000 in your startup. The Opportunity Cost is what you could have earned by investing that money elsewhere, such as stocks or savings. Considering this helps you weigh risks and rewards.

How to Evaluate Opportunity Costs

1. Identify What You're Giving Up:

Think about what you could have done with the time, money, or resources you're using.

2. Compare the Benefits:

Ask: *Does this choice provide more value than the alternative?*

3. Consider Long-Term Impacts:

Short-term gains might have long-term costs. Look at the bigger picture.

4. Be Honest About Sacrifices:

Don't ignore trade-offs just because they're uncomfortable to face.

Everyday Example of Opportunity Cost

Imagine you're deciding between spending a Saturday working overtime or attending a family event.

- Working earns extra income.

- Attending the event strengthens relationships and creates memories.

Weighing the Opportunity Cost ensures your choice aligns with your priorities.

Common Pitfalls in Opportunity Cost

1. Ignoring Non-Monetary Costs:

Opportunity Cost isn't just financial—time, energy, and relationships matter too.

2. Overlooking Hidden Trade-Offs:

Think deeply about what you're sacrificing. Some costs aren't obvious at first.

3. Paralysis by Analysis:

Don't overthink every small decision. Reserve this model for significant choices.

4. Failing to Reassess Priorities:

Your values and goals may change over time. Re-evaluate Opportunity Costs regularly.

Practical Tip: Use "If I Choose This, I Lose That" Thinking

Before making a decision, state clearly what you're giving up. This keeps trade-offs in focus.

Takeaway

Opportunity Cost helps you see the hidden sacrifices behind every choice. It ensures your decisions align with your goals and values.

Life is full of trade-offs — this model ensures you choose wisely. Let's continue refining decision-making tools in the next section.

Chapter 24: The Pareto Principle (80/20 Rule)

What is the Pareto Principle (80/20 Rule)?

In the Pareto Principle, 80% of results come from 20% of efforts. It highlights the imbalance between effort and output, suggesting you should focus on the small actions that create the biggest impact.

This principle applies to almost everything — business, personal goals, relationships, and productivity.

Why the Pareto Principle Matters

Most people waste time on tasks that have little impact. The Pareto Principle helps you prioritize what truly drives success.

For example:

- 20% of your customers often generate 80% of your revenue.

- 20% of your habits likely create 80% of your progress.

Focusing on the critical 20% multiplies your results.

Example: Improving Study Efficiency

Imagine you're preparing for an exam.

- Without the Pareto Principle: You study all topics equally, wasting time on less important ones.

- Using the 80/20 Rule: You identify the 20% of topics most likely to be tested and focus on mastering those.

This targeted approach maximizes your efficiency.

How to Use the Pareto Principle

1. Identify Key Inputs:

Ask: *What 20% of my efforts drive 80% of my results?*

2. Eliminate Low-Impact Tasks:

Stop spending time on things that don't significantly contribute to your goals.

3. Focus on High-Leverage Activities:

Double down on the tasks, relationships, or habits that produce the most value.

4. Regularly Reassess:

Priorities change over time. Keep identifying the most impactful 20%.

Everyday Example of the Pareto Principle

Suppose you're decluttering your home.

- 80% of the clutter comes from 20% of your items. Focus on clearing those items first, and you'll make the biggest difference with minimal effort.

Common Pitfalls in the Pareto Principle

1. Ignoring the Remaining 80%:

While 20% drives most results, the remaining 80% may still matter in some contexts. Don't neglect it entirely.

2. Overgeneralizing:

The ratio isn't always 80/20. Focus on the concept, not the exact numbers.

3. Failing to Identify Priorities:

Without clear priorities, you'll struggle to know where to focus.

4. Misinterpreting the Rule:

It doesn't mean working less—it means working smarter.

Practical Tip: Ask, "What Few Things Make the Biggest Impact?"

Before tackling any goal, identify the small actions that will drive the most significant results.

Takeaway

The Pareto Principle teaches you to prioritize the few efforts that create the most impact. By focusing on the critical 20%, you can achieve more with less.

Understanding value is important, but diminishing returns can set limits. Let's explore this further.

Chapter 25: Marginal Utility

What is Marginal Utility?

Marginal Utility explains how the value or satisfaction from consuming something decreases as you get more of it. The first slice of pizza is amazing, but by the third or fourth, the excitement fades.

This concept is key for making decisions about resources, showing that more isn't always better.

Why Marginal Utility Matters

Understanding Marginal Utility helps you allocate time, money, or energy wisely. It prevents waste by focusing on when additional effort no longer adds value.

For example:

- Studying for an exam for 2 hours might be productive, but studying for 10 hours straight could lead to burnout with little additional learning.

Example: Watching TV

One episode of your favorite show feels relaxing. But binge-watching all night leaves you feeling tired and less satisfied. Marginal Utility explains why balance matters.

How to Use Marginal Utility

1. Identify Diminishing Returns:

Pay attention to when extra effort, money, or time adds less value.

2. Set Limits:

Stop investing once you reach the point where additional input doesn't significantly improve outcomes.

3. Prioritize Quality Over Quantity:

Focus on high-value experiences or resources instead of accumulating more.

4. Evaluate Alternatives:

When Marginal Utility decreases, shift your resources to other areas with higher returns.

Everyday Example of Marginal Utility

Suppose you're shopping for clothes.

- The first few items you buy may be exciting, but buying too many leads to clutter without much extra satisfaction.

Common Pitfalls in Marginal Utility

1. Ignoring the Decline:

Continuing to invest resources after satisfaction decreases leads to waste.

2. Overvaluing Quantity:

More isn't always better—focus on quality and purpose.

3. Not Setting Priorities:

Without clear goals, it's hard to notice when returns start diminishing.

4. Neglecting Alternatives:

When returns decline, explore other opportunities for growth or satisfaction.

Practical Tip: Look for the "Saturation Point"

For any activity, ask: *At what point does more stop adding value?* Use this to set limits.

Takeaway

Marginal Utility helps you understand when "enough is enough." It ensures your resources are used efficiently by focusing on value, not volume.

From here, let's examine how emotions influence decisions.

Chapter 26: Loss Aversion

What is Loss Aversion?

Loss Aversion is the tendency to fear losses more than valuing equivalent gains. For example, losing $10 feels worse than the joy of gaining $10.

This cognitive bias can lead to overly cautious decisions, missed opportunities, or clinging to bad investments.

Why Loss Aversion Matters

Fear of loss often leads people to avoid risks, even when potential rewards are greater. Recognizing this bias helps you make rational, balanced choices.

For example:

- Investors hold onto failing stocks to avoid feeling the pain of selling at a loss.

- A person avoids asking for a raise because they fear rejection.

Awareness of Loss Aversion keeps emotions from driving decisions.

Example: Canceling a Membership

You're hesitant to cancel a gym membership you rarely use because you feel it's a waste of money. Loss Aversion keeps you stuck, even though canceling saves you in the long run.

How to Overcome Loss Aversion

1. Reframe the Situation:

Focus on potential gains instead of losses. Ask: *What do I stand to gain by letting this go?*

2. Consider the Bigger Picture:

Think about long-term benefits versus short-term discomfort.

3. Use Objective Data:

Analyze decisions logically, not emotionally. Numbers often counteract fear.

4. Set Clear Goals:

Align decisions with your goals to minimize the emotional pull of losses.

Everyday Example of Loss Aversion

Imagine hesitating to donate old clothes because you spent money on them. Recognizing Loss Aversion helps you realize that keeping unused items isn't adding value to your life.

Common Pitfalls in Loss Aversion

1. Holding Onto Bad Investments:

Sunk costs can cloud judgment. Focus on future potential, not past losses.

2. Avoiding Risks Unnecessarily:

Over-caution leads to missed opportunities.

3. Overvaluing What You Have:

Just because you own something doesn't mean it's worth keeping.

4. Letting Emotions Dominate Decisions:

Balance emotional responses with logic to make smarter choices.

Practical Tip: Ask, "What Do I Gain by Letting Go?"

Reframing decisions helps you see past the emotional fear of losing.

Takeaway

Loss Aversion reminds you that fear of loss can distort decision-making. By recognizing this bias, you can focus on potential gains and make clearer, more confident choices.

	Urgent	Not Urgent
Important	Do these immediately	Schedule these for later
Not Important	Delegate these	Eliminate these

Chapter 27: The Eisenhower Matrix

What is the Eisenhower Matrix?

The Eisenhower Matrix is a time-management tool that helps you prioritize tasks based on urgency and importance. It divides tasks into four categories:

1. Urgent and Important: Do these immediately.

2. Important but Not Urgent: Schedule these for later.

3. Urgent but Not Important: Delegate these.

4. Not Urgent and Not Important: Eliminate these.

This model ensures you spend your time on what truly matters instead of reacting to distractions.

Why the Eisenhower Matrix Matters

Without clear priorities, you risk wasting time on tasks that feel urgent but add little value. The Eisenhower Matrix helps you focus on meaningful work while minimizing distractions.

For example:

- Answering urgent emails feels productive but might not align with your bigger goals.

- Spending time on important but not urgent activities, like planning or learning, creates long-term success.

Example: Planning a Workday

Suppose you're overwhelmed with tasks: preparing a presentation, responding to emails, and cleaning your desk.

- **Urgent and Important:** Finalizing the presentation.

- **Important but Not Urgent:** Organizing your long-term project goals.

- **Urgent but Not Important:** Responding to minor emails (delegate).

- **Not Urgent and Not Important:** Cleaning your desk (eliminate).

This approach helps you focus on the presentation while scheduling the rest.

How to Use the Eisenhower Matrix

1. List All Your Tasks:

Write down everything you need to do.

2. Sort Tasks Into Categories:

Use the four quadrants to classify each task by urgency and importance.

3. Focus on Quadrant 1:

Tackle urgent and important tasks first.

4. Schedule Quadrant 2:

Plan time for important but not urgent tasks—they're often the most valuable.

Example of the Eisenhower Matrix

Imagine you're juggling personal and professional responsibilities.

- **Urgent and Important:** Paying overdue bills.

- **Important but Not Urgent:** Planning a family vacation.

- **Urgent but Not Important:** Answering a non-critical text.

- **Not Urgent and Not Important:** Scrolling through social media.

Using the matrix ensures your time is spent wisely.

Common Pitfalls in the Eisenhower Matrix

1. Overloading Quadrant 1:

Too many "urgent" tasks indicate poor planning. Focus on Quadrant 2 to prevent last-minute crises.

2. Ignoring Quadrant 2:

Skipping important but not urgent tasks leads to long-term problems.

3. Misclassifying Tasks:

Be honest about what's truly important versus what just feels urgent.

4. Failing to Delegate:

Don't hesitate to assign tasks in Quadrant 3 to others.

Practical Tip: Review Your Matrix Daily

At the start of each day, revisit your matrix to adjust priorities and stay on track.

Takeaway

The Eisenhower Matrix helps you focus on what truly matters by separating urgency from importance. It's a simple yet powerful tool to align your actions with your goals.

Next, let's analyze decision-making even further.

Chapter 28: SWOT Analysis

What is SWOT Analysis?

SWOT Analysis is a framework for evaluating any situation according to:

- **Strengths:** What advantages do you have?

- **Weaknesses:** Where are your limitations?

- **Opportunities:** What external factors can you leverage?

- **Threats:** What risks could derail you?

This model helps you make informed decisions by considering internal and external factors.

Why SWOT Analysis Matters

Rushing into decisions without evaluating all angles can lead to failure. SWOT Analysis forces you to think strategically, balancing opportunities with risks.

For example:

- A business launching a new product might analyze strengths (innovative design), weaknesses (limited budget), opportunities (growing market), and threats (competition).

This framework ensures nothing is overlooked.

Example: Choosing a Career Move

You're deciding whether to switch jobs.

- **Strengths:** Your skills align with the new role.

- **Weaknesses:** You're unfamiliar with the industry.

- **Opportunities:** The new job offers better growth prospects.

- **Threats:** Leaving your current job might risk stability.

By analyzing all factors, you can make a confident choice.

How to Conduct a SWOT Analysis

1. Identify Strengths:

List your internal advantages, like skills, resources, or support systems.

2. Acknowledge Weaknesses:

Be honest about areas where you're lacking.

3. Spot Opportunities:

Look for external factors that can help you succeed, like trends or resources.

4. Prepare for Threats:

Anticipate challenges and plan how to handle them.

Everyday Example of SWOT Analysis

Suppose you're deciding whether to start a fitness routine.

- **Strengths:** You have time in the evenings.

- **Weaknesses:** You struggle with consistency.

- **Opportunities:** A nearby gym offers discounts.

- **Threats:** Work commitments might interfere.

SWOT Analysis helps you create a realistic, actionable plan.

Common Pitfalls in SWOT Analysis

1. Overemphasizing Strengths:

Don't let confidence blind you to weaknesses or risks.

2. Ignoring External Factors:

Opportunities and threats are just as important as internal factors.

3. Being Too Vague:

Specific details make SWOT more effective.

4. Failing to Act on Insights:

SWOT is a planning tool, but its value lies in taking action.

Practical Tip: Use SWOT for Major Decisions

Whenever faced with a big choice, use SWOT to clarify your options and identify the best path forward.

Takeaway

SWOT Analysis is a versatile tool for making strategic decisions. By balancing strengths, weaknesses, opportunities, and threats, you gain a clearer understanding of any situation.

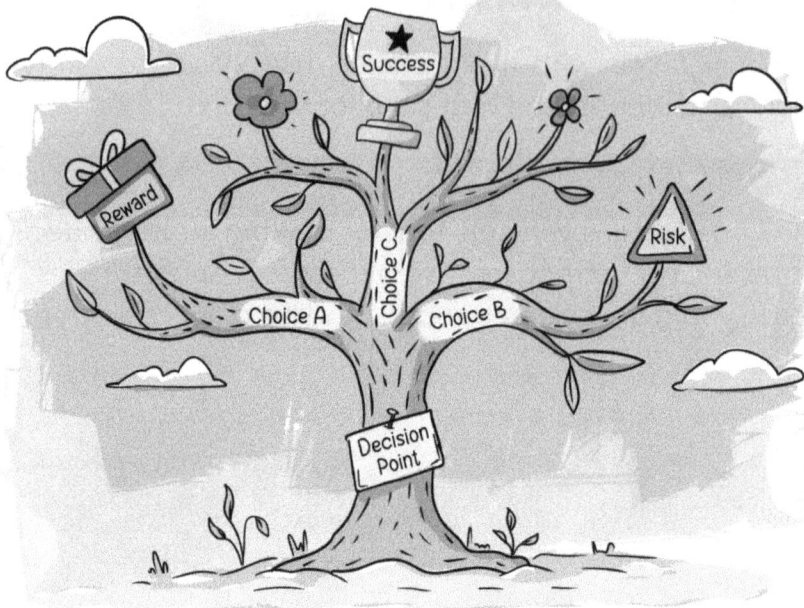

Chapter 29: Decision Trees

What is a Decision Tree?

A Decision Tree is a visual tool for mapping out choices and their possible outcomes. It helps you break down complex decisions step-by-step, weighing risks, rewards, and probabilities.

This model is particularly useful when decisions have multiple layers.

Why Decision Trees Matter

When faced with complex choices, it's easy to feel overwhelmed. A Decision Tree simplifies the process by organizing your options and showing the potential consequences of each path.

For example:

- A company deciding to launch a product might use a Decision Tree to evaluate outcomes like profitability, costs, and market response.

- An individual planning a career change can map options, including potential risks and rewards.

Example: Choosing Between Job Offers

Imagine you're deciding between staying at your current job or accepting a new offer.

- Current job: Stability (high probability), limited growth.

- New offer: High growth potential (medium probability), risk of instability.

A Decision Tree helps you compare these outcomes visually, so you can make a more informed choice.

How to Use a Decision Tree

1. Identify the Decision:

Write down the key choice you need to make.

2. List Options:

Outline all possible actions you could take.

3. Map Outcomes:

For each option, list possible results, including both positive and negative scenarios.

4. Assign Probabilities and Values:

Estimate how likely each outcome is and what its impact would be (e.g., financial, emotional).

5. Analyze the Best Path:

Calculate which option offers the highest overall value or lowest risk.

Everyday Example of a Decision Tree

Imagine you're deciding whether to take an umbrella before heading out.

- Option 1: Take the umbrella. Outcome: Stay dry if it rains but carry extra weight if it doesn't.

- Option 2: Don't take the umbrella. Outcome: Stay light, but risk getting wet.

Mapping these options visually helps you weigh the probabilities and make the right call.

Common Pitfalls in Decision Trees

1. Overcomplicating the Tree:

Too many branches make the tree hard to interpret. Focus on the most important choices.

2. Guessing Probabilities:

Be realistic and use available data whenever possible.

3. Ignoring Emotional Factors:

Decision Trees focus on logic but should include emotional impacts where relevant.

4. Skipping Follow-Up Decisions:

Account for how each choice could lead to new decisions down the line.

Practical Tip: Start Simple

Begin with one main decision and a few branches. Add more detail only if necessary.

Takeaway

Decision Trees help you structure choices and visualize outcomes, making complex decisions clearer and more manageable.

When your choices depend on others' actions, understanding their strategies is crucial. Let's explore this next.

Chapter 30: Game Theory

What is Game Theory?

Game Theory analyzes decision-making in situations where the outcome depends on the actions of others. It's about understanding how your choices interact with theirs, whether you're competing or collaborating.

This model is used in business negotiations, politics, economics, and everyday interactions.

Why Game Theory Matters

In many decisions, your success isn't determined by your actions alone — it depends on how others respond. Game Theory helps you anticipate their moves and choose strategies that maximize your outcomes.

For example:

- Companies setting prices must consider how competitors will react.

- Friends deciding where to meet for dinner must weigh preferences and compromises.

Example: The Prisoner's Dilemma

Two suspects are arrested and interrogated separately. They can either cooperate by staying silent or betray the other for a lighter sentence.

- If both stay silent, they get minor sentences.

- If one betrays the other, the betrayer goes free while the other gets a heavy sentence.

- If both betray, they both receive moderate sentences.

Game Theory shows that trust and collaboration often lead to better outcomes than selfishness.

How to Use Game Theory

1. Understand the Players:

Identify everyone involved and their potential strategies.

2. Predict Their Goals:

Consider what others want and how they might act to achieve it.

3. Evaluate Your Options:

Think about how your choices will influence others and vice versa.

4. Choose the Best Strategy:

Select the option that maximizes your benefit while accounting for others' actions.

Everyday Example of Game Theory

Imagine splitting the bill at dinner.

- If everyone orders moderately, the bill is fair.
- If one person splurges while expecting the group to split evenly, others might feel cheated.

Game Theory helps you navigate these dynamics and encourage fair collaboration.

Common Pitfalls in Game Theory

1. Assuming Others Are Predictable:

People's choices can be influenced by emotions or unexpected factors.

2. Ignoring Collaboration Opportunities:

Not all situations are competitions. Cooperation often leads to better outcomes.

3. Focusing Only on Short-Term Wins:

Strategies that work now might hurt relationships or trust in the long run.

4. Overthinking Simple Situations:

Not every decision requires complex strategy. Use Game Theory for significant choices.

Practical Tip: Think Like the Other Player

Before making a choice, ask: *What would I do in their position?* This helps you anticipate their actions.

Takeaway

Game Theory helps you navigate decisions where outcomes depend on others' strategies. Whether competing or collaborating, it equips you to make smarter, more strategic choices.

From decisions to problem-solving, understanding root causes is essential. Let's take a further look.

Problem Solving Models

Chapter 31: Root Cause Analysis

What is Root Cause Analysis?

Root Cause Analysis is a problem-solving method that focuses on identifying the true source of an issue rather than just treating its symptoms. It's about digging deeper to ask: *What is really causing this problem?*

By addressing the root cause, you solve the problem permanently instead of applying temporary fixes.

Why Root Cause Analysis Matters

Most people fix surface-level issues without understanding their origins. This leads to recurring problems and wasted effort. Root Cause Analysis ensures you address the core issue, saving time and resources.

For example:

- A machine breaks down. Fixing it restores function temporarily, but analyzing why it broke (e.g., poor maintenance) prevents future breakdowns.

Example: Customer Complaints

Imagine a business faces frequent complaints about slow service.

- Symptom: Long wait times.

- Root Cause: Insufficient staffing during peak hours.

By addressing the staffing issue, the company reduces wait times and complaints.

How to Perform Root Cause Analysis

1. Define the Problem:

Be specific about what's happening. Avoid vague descriptions.

2. Ask "Why" Repeatedly:

Use the 5 Whys Technique (e.g., *Why did this happen? And why did that happen?*) to uncover deeper layers.

3. Identify the Root Cause:

Look for patterns or systemic issues causing the problem.

4. Develop a Long-Term Solution:

Focus on eliminating the root cause, not just managing symptoms.

Everyday Example of Root Cause Analysis

Suppose you're constantly late to work.

- Symptom: You miss the bus.

- Root Cause: You're waking up too late.

- Solution: Set an earlier alarm to avoid the rush entirely.

Addressing the root saves you from repeated stress and delays.

Common Pitfalls in Root Cause Analysis

1. Stopping Too Soon:

Surface answers often hide deeper problems. Keep asking "why" to dig further.

2. Focusing on Blame:

Avoid assigning blame to people. Focus on processes or systems instead.

3. Overlooking Patterns:

Recurring problems often point to root causes. Don't treat them as isolated incidents.

4. Failing to Act on Insights:

Identifying the root cause 'is useless without implementing a solution.

Practical Tip: Look for the Chain Reaction

Most problems result from a series of events. Trace each link backward until you reach the starting point.

Takeaway

Root Cause Analysis helps you solve problems permanently by targeting their origins. It's a powerful tool for creating long-lasting improvements.

Let's continue exploring solutions with fresh perspectives.

Chapter 32: The 5 Whys Technique

What is the 5 Whys Technique?

The 5 Whys Technique is a simple problem-solving method where you repeatedly ask "Why?" to uncover the root cause of an issue. Each answer leads you closer to the underlying problem.

It's based on the idea that surface-level issues often have deeper causes. Asking "why" helps you dig past symptoms to find solutions that stick.

Why the 5 Whys Technique Matters

Problems rarely happen in isolation — they're often symptoms of larger issues. The 5 Whys Technique prevents you from stopping at superficial answers.

For example:

- A missed deadline might seem like the problem. But asking "why" reveals deeper issues like unclear instructions or poor time management.

Example: A Leaking Roof

Problem: The roof is leaking.

1. **Why?** The shingles are damaged.

2. **Why?** They weren't replaced on time.

3. **Why?** The maintenance schedule wasn't followed.

4. **Why?** The team didn't know about the schedule.

5. **Why?** There's no system for tracking tasks.

Root Cause: Lack of a task-tracking system.

How to Use the 5 Whys Technique

1. Start with the Problem:

Clearly define the issue you're trying to solve.

2. Ask "Why" Five Times:

Each answer should lead to the next "why." Keep going until you reach the root cause.

3. Focus on Processes, Not People:

Look for flaws in systems or workflows, not individual blame.

4. Develop a Solution:

Once you identify the root cause, design a plan to address it.

Everyday Example of the 5 Whys

Suppose your car won't start.

1. Why? The battery is dead.

2. Why? I left the lights on.

3. Why? I forgot to turn them off.

4. Why? I was in a rush.

5. Why? I didn't allow enough time to leave.

Solution: Set a reminder to check the lights before leaving the car.

Common Pitfalls in the 5 Whys Technique

1. Stopping Too Soon:

The first "why" rarely reveals the true root cause. Keep digging.

2. Jumping to Conclusions:

Avoid guessing answers without evidence.

3. Focusing on Blame:

This technique is about fixing systems, not pointing fingers.

4. Ignoring Complexity:

Some problems have multiple root causes. Be open to finding more than one.

Practical Tip: Involve Others

When using the 5 Whys, gather input from people who understand the problem. Different perspectives reveal hidden causes.

Takeaway

The 5 Whys Technique simplifies problem-solving by breaking issues into smaller pieces. It's a practical way to uncover the root cause and build effective solutions.

Let's continue uncovering creative approaches to problem-solving.

Chapter 33: Lateral Thinking

What is Lateral Thinking?

Lateral Thinking is the ability to solve problems creatively by approaching them from unexpected angles. Instead of following traditional methods, you think outside the box.

This model is especially useful when conventional thinking has failed or when a fresh perspective is needed.

Why Lateral Thinking Matters

Humans often default to familiar patterns, which can limit creativity. Lateral Thinking breaks those patterns, unlocking innovative ideas.

For example:

- Instead of improving a clunky product design, Lateral Thinking might suggest eliminating the need for the product entirely.

Example: Solving Office Clutter

A company struggles with messy desks.

- Conventional Thinking: Add more storage space.
- Lateral Thinking: Shift to a paperless office, removing the need for physical storage altogether.

The creative approach solves the problem at its source.

How to Use Lateral Thinking

1. Question Assumptions:

Ask: *What if this rule didn't exist?* Break free from "how things are done."

2. Generate Wild Ideas:

Think of unconventional solutions without worrying if they're practical at first.

3. Combine Unrelated Ideas:

Look for inspiration in other fields or industries.

4. Reframe the Problem:

Instead of asking How do I fix this? ask How can I make this irrelevant?

Everyday Example of Lateral Thinking

Suppose you need to transport groceries without a car.

- Conventional Thinking: Find a ride.

- Lateral Thinking: Use a delivery service or switch to online shopping.

Thinking outside the box often leads to simpler, more effective solutions.

Common Pitfalls in Lateral Thinking

1. Dismissing Ideas Too Quickly:

Even wild ideas can spark useful insights. Explore them fully before rejecting them.

2. Clinging to Tradition:

Familiar methods feel safe but may not solve the problem.

3. Overcomplicating Solutions:

Simplicity is often the hallmark of great lateral ideas.

4. Ignoring Feedback:

Innovative ideas still need to be tested and refined with input from others.

Practical Tip: Ask "What If?"

For any problem, ask questions like *What if we did the opposite? What if this rule didn't exist?* These shifts often lead to creative breakthroughs.

Takeaway

Lateral Thinking helps you escape mental ruts and uncover innovative solutions. It's a mindset that encourages creativity and reinvention.

Let's continue exploring tools for simplifying and clarifying complex ideas.

Chapter 34: The Feynman Technique

What is The Feynman Technique?

The Feynman Technique describes mastering complex ideas by breaking them down into simple terms. Named after physicist Richard Feynman, it's based on the idea that if you can't explain something simply, you don't truly understand it.

This model combines learning and teaching to deepen comprehension.

Why The Feynman Technique Matters

Complicated explanations often hides shallow understanding. By forcing yourself to simplify concepts, you uncover gaps in your knowledge and fill them effectively.

For example:

- A teacher explaining physics without jargon ensures both they and their students truly grasp the material.

Example: Learning Budgeting

You're learning how to manage finances.

- Without Feynman: Memorize formulas without understanding them.
- With Feynman: Teach someone else how budgeting works, revealing gaps in your knowledge that need clarification.

Teaching strengthens your own understanding.

How to Use The Feynman Technique

1. Pick a Concept:

Choose something you want to learn or explain.

2. Write It Simply:

Break it down into terms a child could understand. Avoid jargon.

3. Identify Gaps:

Notice where your explanation feels unclear. Study those areas again.

4. Refine and Repeat:

Rewrite your explanation until it's simple and complete.

Everyday Example of The Feynman Technique

Suppose you're learning how solar panels work.

- Start by explaining: *They turn sunlight into electricity.*

- Dive deeper: *How does that happen? Through something called photovoltaic cells.*

- Simplify further: *These cells capture sunlight and turn it into energy we can use.*

Each layer improves your understanding.

Common Pitfalls in The Feynman Technique

1. Using Jargon:

Complex terms hide gaps in understanding. Stick to plain language.

2. Skipping the Gaps:

Don't avoid areas you don't fully understand—those are where learning happens.

3. Overcomplicating Explanations:

Keep your explanations short and focused on essentials.

4. Ignoring Feedback:

Test your explanation on others to ensure it's clear.

Practical Tip: Pretend You're Teaching a Child

When explaining a concept, imagine your audience is a curious child. Their questions will force you to simplify and clarify.

Takeaway

The Feynman Technique turns learning into teaching, helping you master even the most complex ideas. It's a tool for clarity, focus, and deep understanding.

Let's continue exploring practical shortcuts to tackle everyday problems.

Chapter 35: Heuristic Problem Solving

What is Heuristic Problem Solving?

Heuristics are mental shortcuts or "rules of thumb" that simplify problem-solving. Instead of analyzing every detail, you use quick, practical methods to make decisions or find solutions.

While not always perfect, heuristics save time and effort in everyday situations.

Why Heuristic Problem Solving Matters

Humans often face decisions with limited time or information. Heuristics allow you to act quickly without overthinking, especially when perfection isn't necessary.

For example:

- When choosing a restaurant, you might rely on the heuristic *Pick the one with the best reviews,* rather than researching all options exhaustively.

Example: Packing for a Trip

Instead of overanalyzing what to pack, you use a heuristic like *Pack for three days, regardless of trip length.* This simplifies decision-making and saves time.

How to Use Heuristics

1. Define the Problem:

Be clear about what you need to solve or decide.

2. Pick a Rule of Thumb:

Use a simple guideline that fits the situation, like *Go with the majority opinion* or *Follow what worked last time.*

3. Evaluate Results:

Check if the heuristic worked well. Adjust if needed.

4. Combine Heuristics for Complex Problems:

Use multiple rules to address different aspects of the issue.

Everyday Example of Heuristics

Suppose you're grocery shopping on a budget.

- Heuristic: *Choose the store-brand version to save money.*

- This shortcut eliminates the need to compare every price, simplifying your decision.

1. Overreliance on Shortcuts:

Heuristics aren't foolproof. Use them for quick decisions, not critical ones.

2. Applying the Wrong Rule:

Not all heuristics fit every situation. Choose appropriately.

3. Ignoring Details:

While details aren't always critical, missing key ones can lead to mistakes.

4. Resisting Feedback:

Adjust heuristics based on results to improve their effectiveness.

Practical Tip: Test and Adjust

After using a heuristic, evaluate its success. Keep refining your shortcuts for better results over time.

Takeaway

Heuristic Problem Solving helps you act efficiently by simplifying decisions. It's a practical tool for navigating everyday challenges with ease.

Let's continue exploring methods that combine experimentation with observation.

Chapter 36: The Scientific Method

What is The Scientific Method?

The Scientific Method is a systematic way to solve problems by asking questions, testing hypotheses, and analyzing results. It's about learning through experimentation and evidence, not guesswork or assumptions.

This model ensures that your conclusions are based on facts, not bias or opinion.

Why The Scientific Method Matters

Humans often jump to conclusions without testing their ideas. The Scientific Method slows you down, forcing you to gather evidence and evaluate results before deciding.

For example:

- Instead of assuming a new diet will work, you track its impact on your health over time.

Example: Testing a Study Strategy

You wonder if studying in the morning improves focus.

- **Question:** Does morning study improve focus?

- **Hypothesis:** Studying in the morning increases focus by 20%.

- **Experiment:** Study in the morning for one week and at night for another.

- **Observation:** Measure focus levels during both weeks.

- **Conclusion:** Morning study improves focus by 15%, supporting your hypothesis.

This process helps you make informed decisions based on evidence.

How to Use The Scientific Method

1. Ask a Question:

Start with a clear, focused problem or curiosity.

2. Form a Hypothesis:

Make an educated guess about the outcome.

3. Design an Experiment:

Create a testable plan to gather data.

4. Analyze Results:

Look for patterns or evidence that confirm or disprove your hypothesis.

5. Draw a Conclusion:

Use the results to answer your question. If the hypothesis was wrong, revise and test again.

Everyday Example of The Scientific Method

Suppose you want to reduce stress.

- **Question:** Does daily meditation lower stress?

- **Hypothesis:** Meditation reduces stress by 30%.

- **Experiment:** Meditate daily for two weeks and track stress levels.

- **Observation:** Stress decreased by 25%.

- **Conclusion:** Meditation is effective, but results vary slightly from your hypothesis.

The process gives you clear, actionable insights.

Common Pitfalls in The Scientific Method

1. Skipping the Hypothesis:

Without a clear guess, you can't measure success accurately.

2. Ignoring Variables:

Controlling factors like time, place, or method ensures reliable results.

3. Drawing Conclusions Too Early:

Wait for complete data before deciding.

4. Fearing Failure:

A disproven hypothesis isn't a failure—it's a step toward better understanding.

Practical Tip: Keep It Simple

Start with small, manageable experiments. Complex setups can lead to confusion or unreliable results.

Takeaway

The Scientific Method helps you solve problems with evidence and logic. It's a structured approach that turns curiosity into actionable knowledge.

Let's continue reviewing tools for reasoning and explanation.

Chapter 37: Abductive Reasoning

What is Abductive Reasoning?

Abductive Reasoning is the process of finding the most likely explanation for a set of observations. It's often called "inference to the best explanation."

Unlike deductive reasoning (which proves conclusions) or inductive reasoning (which generalizes patterns), abductive reasoning is about making the best guess when faced with incomplete information.

Why Abductive Reasoning Matters

In real life, you rarely have all the facts. Abductive Reasoning helps you make logical decisions despite uncertainty.

For example:

- If you hear water dripping, you might work out that a faucet is leaking, even without seeing it.

Example: Diagnosing a Problem

Your car won't start.

- Observation: The engine won't turn over, and the lights are dim.

- Likely Explanation: The battery is dead.

This reasoning guides you toward a solution without needing every detail upfront.

How to Use Abductive Reasoning

1. Gather Observations:

List the facts or clues available.

2. Generate Possible Explanations:

Brainstorm reasons that could explain the observations.

3. Choose the Most Likely Explanation:

Pick the explanation that fits best, given the evidence.

4. Test and Adjust:

Act on your reasoning and gather more data if needed.

Everyday Example of Abductive Reasoning

Suppose you smell smoke in the kitchen.

- Possible Explanations: A dish is burning, a candle is out of control, or something outside is on fire.

- Most Likely Explanation: The oven is burning food.

This reasoning helps you act quickly to check the oven first.

Common Pitfalls in Abductive Reasoning

1. Jumping to Conclusions:

Avoid settling on an explanation without considering alternatives.

2. Ignoring Unlikely Factors:

While some explanations are improbable, don't rule them out entirely without evidence.

3. Confirmation Bias:

Be careful not to favor explanations that match your assumptions.

4. Overcomplicating the Problem:

Stick to the simplest, most logical explanation first.

Practical Tip: Use Occam's Razor

When choosing between explanations, prefer the simplest one that fits the evidence.

Takeaway

Abductive Reasoning helps you navigate uncertainty by finding the best explanation for incomplete information. It's a practical tool for decision-making and problem-solving.

Let's look at further solutions that put human needs at the center.

Chapter 38: Design Thinking

What is Design Thinking?

Design Thinking is a human-centered approach to solving problems. It focuses on understanding user needs, brainstorming creative ideas, and testing solutions.

This model emphasizes empathy, collaboration, and adaptability, making it ideal for creating products, services, or processes that truly work for people.

Why Design Thinking Matters

Traditional problem-solving often skips empathy, leading to solutions that miss the mark. Design Thinking ensures your approach aligns with real user needs.

For example:

- A company redesigning a website uses Design Thinking to focus on making navigation easier for users instead of just adding flashy features.

Example: Improving Public Transport

Imagine you're tasked with improving a bus system.

- Empathize: Talk to passengers about their frustrations.

- Define: Identify the core issue—long wait times.

- Ideate: Brainstorm solutions like more buses or a real-time tracking app.

- Prototype: Create a basic app to test.

- Test: Gather feedback and refine the app based on user input.

This process ensures practical, user-friendly results.

How to Apply Design Thinking

1. Empathize:

Understand the user's perspective through interviews or observation.

2. Define the Problem:

Clearly state the issue based on user insights.

3. Ideate Solutions:

Brainstorm as many creative ideas as possible.

4. Prototype:

Build simple, testable versions of your ideas.

5. Test and Refine:

Use feedback to improve your solution iteratively.

Everyday Example of Design Thinking

Suppose you're organizing a family dinner.

- Empathize: Ask family members about dietary preferences.
- Define: The goal is to serve a meal everyone enjoys.
- Ideate: Brainstorm menu ideas.
- Prototype: Test one dish before finalizing the menu.
- Test: Get feedback and adjust if needed.

This ensures everyone has a great experience.

Common Pitfalls in Design Thinking

1. Skipping Empathy:

Solving a problem without understanding user needs leads to ineffective solutions.

2. Rushing Prototypes:

Prototypes should be simple but meaningful.

3. Resisting Feedback:

Iteration is key — be willing to revise your ideas.

4. Overthinking Ideation:

Focus on generating ideas, not perfection, during brainstorming.

Practical Tip: Use Rapid Prototyping

Quickly test ideas with basic models or mock-ups. Feedback from early prototypes often leads to breakthrough solutions.

Takeaway

Design Thinking ensures solutions are practical, creative, and human-centered. It's a flexible approach that adapts to real needs through empathy and iteration.

Let's look at more ways to test assumptions.

Chapter 39: Hypothesis Testing

What is Hypothesis Testing?

Hypothesis Testing is the process of creating a statement about a possible outcome and then testing it to see if it is true. It's a way to validate assumptions using data, experiments, or observations.

This model ensures decisions are based on evidence, not guesses.

Why Hypothesis Testing Matters

Assumptions can lead to costly mistakes if they're wrong. Hypothesis Testing forces you to evaluate ideas objectively, minimizing risk and maximizing results.

For example:

- A business tests whether offering free shipping increases sales. Instead of assuming, they collect data to confirm or disprove the idea.

Example: Testing a New Marketing Strategy

You want to know if posting daily on social media increases engagement.

- Hypothesis: Daily posts will boost engagement by 25%.

- Test: Post daily for two weeks and measure engagement levels.

- Outcome: Engagement increases by 15%. The hypothesis isn't fully supported, so you refine your approach.

This process ensures data-driven decisions.

How to Conduct Hypothesis Testing

1. Formulate a Hypothesis:

Make a clear, testable statement about what you expect to happen.

2. Design an Experiment:

Create a plan to gather evidence, ensuring it's measurable and reliable.

3. Collect Data:

Observe and record results from the test.

4. Analyze Results:

Compare the data to your hypothesis.

5. Draw Conclusions:

Decide whether the hypothesis is supported, rejected, or needs adjustment.

Everyday Example of Hypothesis Testing

Imagine you're trying to improve sleep by going to bed earlier.

- Hypothesis: Sleeping an hour earlier will reduce daytime fatigue.

- Test: Adjust bedtime for a week and track how you feel during the day.

- Outcome: Fatigue decreases, confirming the hypothesis.

Testing the idea ensures your actions are effective.

Common Pitfalls in Hypothesis Testing

1. Making Vague Hypotheses:

Statements like *Things might improve* are hard to test. Be specific.

2. Using Incomplete Data:

Ensure your sample size is large enough to draw meaningful conclusions.

3. Ignoring Confounding Factors:

External variables can affect results. Control them as much as possible.

4. Forgetting to Iterate:

A single test may not give the full picture. Repeat and refine if needed.

Practical Tip: Always Ask, "How Will I Measure Success?"

Define clear metrics before testing so you can evaluate results objectively.

Takeaway

Hypothesis Testing is a reliable way to validate ideas and make informed decisions. By relying on evidence, you reduce uncertainty and increase your chances of success.

Let's continue exploring ways to compare and refine options effectively.

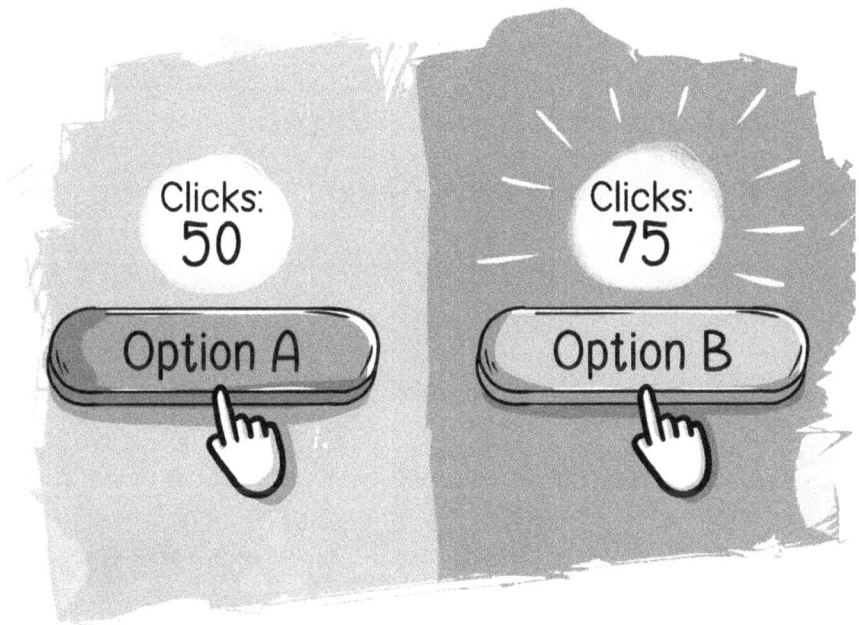

Chapter 40: A/B Testing

What is A/B Testing?

A/B Testing compares two versions of something—like a webpage, ad, or product feature—to see which performs better. It's a practical way to refine decisions by testing options directly with real users.

This model is frequently used in marketing, design, and product development to optimize results.

Why A/B Testing Matters

Guessing which option works best can lead to wasted time and resources. A/B Testing eliminates the guesswork by showing you what actually performs better.

For example:

- A company tests two email subject lines to see which gets more clicks.

Example: Choosing a Website Design

You're deciding between two homepage layouts.

- Option A: Focuses on visuals.

- Option B: Focuses on text.

- Test: Show each version to 1,000 visitors and measure conversions.

- Result: Option B performs 30% better, so you choose it.

A/B Testing ensures data backs your decision.

How to Conduct A/B Testing

1. Define the Variable:

Choose one thing to test, like a headline, color, or layout.

2. Split Your Audience:

Divide users randomly into two groups—one sees Option A, the other Option B.

3. Measure Results:

Track key metrics like clicks, sales, or engagement.

4. Analyze the Data:

Compare the performance of each option.

5. Implement the Winner:

Use the best-performing version and iterate further if needed.

Everyday Example of A/B Testing

Suppose you're organizing a party and debating invitations.

- Option A: A handwritten note.

- Option B: A digital card.

- Test: Send half of your friends Option A and the other half Option B.

- Result: More people respond to the digital card, so you use it.

This simple test guides your choice.

Common Pitfalls in A/B Testing

1. Testing Too Many Variables:

Changing multiple things at once makes it hard to tell what caused the difference.

2. Drawing Conclusions Too Early:

Ensure your sample size is large enough for reliable results.

3. Focusing on the Wrong Metrics:

Track outcomes that align with your goals (e.g., clicks aren't useful if sales are the priority).

4. Failing to Retest:

Repeat tests periodically to ensure results hold over time.

Practical Tip: Start Small

Begin with simple tests, like comparing two headlines, before moving on to larger changes.

Takeaway

A/B Testing helps you make data-driven choices by directly comparing options. It's a practical way to refine strategies and improve outcomes.

Let's further explore strategic frameworks for decision-making and problem-solving.

Strategic Thinking Models

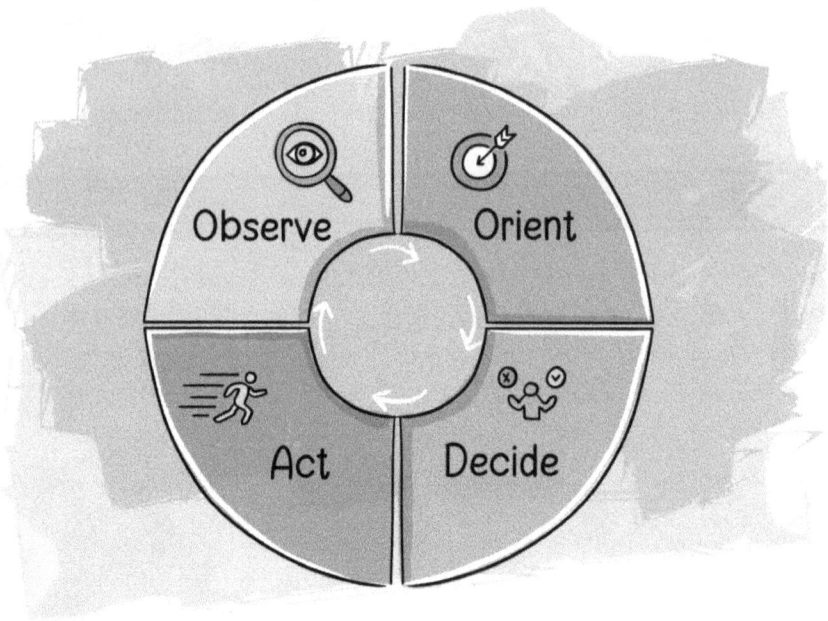

Chapter 41: The OODA Loop

What is the OODA Loop?

The OODA Loop is a decision-making framework developed by military strategist John Boyd. It stands for **Observe, Orient, Decide, Act** and is designed for fast, adaptive decision-making in dynamic situations.

This model is widely used in business, strategy, and problem-solving where speed and flexibility are critical.

Why the OODA Loop Matters

Quick, effective decisions often depend on how well you adapt to changing circumstances. The OODA Loop helps you to continuously reassess the situation and adjust your actions.

For example:

- A company launching a product observes market trends, orients their strategy, decides on a pricing model, and acts by releasing the product—all while monitoring competitor moves.

Example: Adapting to a Traffic Jam

Imagine you're driving and encounter unexpected traffic.

1. Observe: Notice the traffic jam ahead.

2. Orient: Check maps for alternate routes.

3. Decide: Choose the fastest detour.

4. Act: Take the new route.

The loop repeats as you reassess conditions.

How to Use the OODA Loop

1. Observe:

Gather information about your environment. Stay aware of changes and new data.

2. Orient:

Analyze the information and understand its implications. Consider biases or blind spots.

3. Decide:

Choose the best course of action based on your analysis.

4. Act:

Implement your decision quickly, then return to the observation phase to see if adjustments are needed.

Everyday Example of the OODA Loop

Suppose you're planning a weekend hike, and the forecast changes to rain.

- **Observe:** Rain is predicted.

- **Orient:** Evaluate your gear and possible trail conditions.

- **Decide:** Choose a waterproof jacket and an easier trail.

- **Act:** Update your plan and proceed.

The OODA Loop ensures your plan adapts to new conditions.

Common Pitfalls in the OODA Loop

1. Getting Stuck in Observation:

Overanalyzing delays decisions. Act quickly to stay ahead.

2. Ignoring Orientation:

Acting without fully understanding the situation leads to mistakes.

3. Skipping Feedback:

Failing to revisit the observation phase prevents you from adapting to new information.

4. Being Too Rigid:

The loop thrives on flexibility. Adjust as conditions change.

Practical Tip: Act on Imperfect Information

In fast-changing situations, waiting for perfect data can be costly. Use the best information available and refine your actions as you go.

Takeaway

The OODA Loop helps you make fast, adaptive decisions by continuously observing, analyzing, and adjusting. It's a dynamic model for navigating uncertainty with confidence.

Let's continue reviewing structured approaches to anticipating the future.

Chapter 42: Scenario Planning

What is Scenario Planning?

Scenario Planning is the process of imagining and preparing for different possible futures. Instead of predicting one outcome, you explore multiple scenarios and develop plans for each.

This model helps you manage uncertainty by ensuring you're ready for a range of possibilities.

Why Scenario Planning Matters

Life and business are full of unpredictability. Scenario Planning helps you avoid being blindsided by changes by thinking ahead.

For example:

- A company preparing for economic downturns creates plans for maintaining cash flow, cutting costs, and seizing new opportunities.

Example: Planning a Vacation

You're planning a trip but unsure about the weather.

- **Scenario A:** It's sunny—plan outdoor activities.

- **Scenario B:** It's rainy—prepare indoor options.

- **Scenario C:** A storm hits—have a cancellation plan.

By preparing for all scenarios, you ensure a smooth trip regardless of the weather.

How to Use Scenario Planning

1. Identify Key Factors:

Determine the uncertainties that could affect your situation (e.g., weather, market trends).

2. Develop Scenarios:

Imagine best-case, worst-case, and middle-ground outcomes.

3. Plan for Each Scenario:

Create strategies and contingency plans tailored to each possibility.

4. Monitor Key Indicators:

Watch for signs that point toward one scenario becoming more likely.

Everyday Example of Scenario Planning

Suppose you're preparing for a job interview.

- **Scenario A:** The interviewer asks standard questions—practice answers.

- **Scenario B:** The interviewer focuses on problem-solving—review case studies.

- **Scenario C:** The interview runs long—prepare for deeper discussions.

Thinking ahead ensures you're ready for any situation.

Common Pitfalls in Scenario Planning

1. Focusing on Only One Scenario:

Relying on a single prediction leaves you vulnerable to surprises.

2. Ignoring Low-Probability Outcomes:

Even unlikely scenarios can have significant impacts. Prepare for them.

3. Overcomplicating Plans:

Simple, actionable strategies are more effective than overly complex ones.

4. Failing to Revisit Plans:

Scenarios evolve. Regularly update your plans based on new information.

Practical Tip: Use "What If" Thinking

For any situation, ask: *What if this happens? What's my plan?* Thinking through possibilities builds confidence and readiness.

Takeaway

Scenario Planning helps you prepare for uncertainty by anticipating multiple outcomes and creating flexible strategies. It's a powerful way to stay proactive and adaptable.

Let's continue exploring frameworks for playing to your strengths.

Chapter 43: The Hedgehog Concept

What is The Hedgehog Concept?

The Hedgehog Concept, inspired by Jim Collins' book *Good to Great,* focuses on finding the intersection of three areas:

1. **What you're deeply passionate about.**

2. **What you can be the best in the world at.**

3. **What drives your economic or personal success.**

This model helps you identify your core focus — the one thing you can do exceptionally well.

Why The Hedgehog Concept Matters

Spreading yourself too thin across multiple goals dilutes your efforts. The Hedgehog Concept simplifies your priorities, ensuring you focus on what truly matters.

For example:

- A business that excels in logistics might focus solely on supply chain optimization instead of branching into unrelated areas.

Example: Choosing a Career Path

Suppose you're deciding between different careers.

- Passion: You love helping others.

- Talent: You're skilled in communication.

- Success: Counseling offers meaningful work and financial stability.

Becoming a counselor touches on all three areas, making it your "Hedgehog."

How to Apply The Hedgehog Concept

1. Reflect on Your Passions:

Ask: What do I truly love doing?

2. Assess Your Strengths:

Identify areas where you consistently excel or show potential for mastery.

3. Evaluate Impact:

Focus on activities that create measurable success or results.

4. Eliminate Distractions:

Stop pursuing goals that don't align with your Hedgehog Concept.

Everyday Example of The Hedgehog Concept

Imagine you're starting a side business.

- Passion: You enjoy baking.

- Talent: You make excellent cakes.

- Results: Local demand for custom cakes is high.

Focusing on custom cakes aligns with your strengths and drives success.

Common Pitfalls in The Hedgehog Concept

1. Ignoring Passion:

Success without passion often leads to burnout.

2. Overestimating Strengths:

Be honest about what you're truly the best at.

3. Chasing Unrelated Goals:

Activities outside your focus dilute your efforts and results.

4. Neglecting Feedback:

Regularly reassess your Hedgehog Concept based on real-world results.

Practical Tip: Use a Venn Diagram

Draw three overlapping circles for passion, talent, and success. Where they meet is your focus area.

Takeaway

The Hedgehog Concept helps you simplify your goals by focusing on what you're best at and passionate about. It's a blueprint for achieving meaningful success.

Let's further discuss strategic models that balance risk and reward.

Chapter 44: Risk Management

What is Risk Management?

Risk Management is the process of identifying, assessing, and mitigating potential risks to achieve your goals while minimizing negative impacts. Instead of avoiding all risks, it's about finding a balance between taking calculated risks and protecting against failure.

This model applies to everything from business ventures to personal decisions.

Why Risk Management Matters

Every decision involves uncertainty. Risk Management helps you act confidently by preparing for the worst while working toward the best.

For example:

- A company launching a product anticipates risks like competition or supply chain issues and creates contingency plans to address them.

Example: Planning a Big Event

Suppose you're organizing an outdoor wedding.

- Risks: Rain, vendor cancellations, or power outages.

- Mitigation: Rent a tent, have backup vendors, and ensure a generator is available.

By managing risks, you reduce stress and ensure a successful event.

How to Use Risk Management

1. Identify Risks:

List potential problems that could arise.

2. Assess Impact and Likelihood:

For each risk, evaluate how severe it would be and how likely it is to happen.

3. Develop Mitigation Plans:

Create strategies to minimize or respond to risks.

4. Monitor and Adapt:

Keep an eye on risks as circumstances change and adjust plans as needed.

Everyday Example of Risk Management

Imagine you're saving for a vacation.

- Risks: Unexpected expenses (like car repairs) might reduce your savings.

- Mitigation: Create an emergency fund to cover surprise costs.

This approach ensures your vacation budget stays intact even if something goes wrong.

Common Pitfalls in Risk Management

1. Ignoring Small Risks:

Minor risks can escalate if left unaddressed.

2. Overpreparing:

Excessive focus on unlikely risks wastes time and resources.

3. Failing to Reassess:

Risks evolve over time. Regularly update your plans.

4. Avoiding All Risks:

Taking no risks often means missing valuable opportunities.

Practical Tip: Use a Risk Matrix

Plot risks on a matrix with two axes: "Likelihood" and "Impact." Focus on addressing high-impact, high-likelihood risks first.

Takeaway

Risk Management helps you navigate uncertainty with confidence. By balancing risks and rewards, you increase your chances of success while minimizing setbacks.

Let's continue exploring tools for analyzing competition and strategy.

Chapter 45: Competitive Analysis

What is Competitive Analysis?

Competitive Analysis is the process of studying your competitors to identify their strengths, weaknesses, and strategies. This helps you find opportunities to outperform them.

It's a critical tool in business, sports, and any context where success depends on understanding others in the field.

Why Competitive Analysis Matters

Without knowing what others are doing, you risk falling behind or wasting resources on ineffective strategies. Competitive Analysis helps you differentiate yourself and focus on what sets you apart.

For example:

- A start-up launching a new app analyzes competitors' features to identify gaps they can fill, such as better user experience or unique functionality.

Example: Opening a Coffee Shop

You want to stand out from other coffee shops in your area.

- Strengths of Competitors: Popular locations, loyal customers.

- Weaknesses of Competitors: Long wait times, limited menu options.

- Your Opportunity: Offer faster service and unique menu items like locally sourced pastries.

Understanding your competition helps you carve out your niche.

How to Conduct Competitive Analysis

1. Identify Competitors:

List direct and indirect competitors in your space.

2. Analyze Strengths and Weaknesses:

Evaluate what they do well and where they fall short.

3. Find Opportunities:

Look for gaps or unmet needs that you can address.

4. Monitor Regularly:

Keep an eye on competitors' strategies to adapt and stay ahead.

Everyday Example of Competitive Analysis

Suppose you're applying for a job.

- Competitors: Other applicants.

- Their Strengths: Relevant degrees or experience.

- Their Weaknesses: Lack of creativity or unique skills.

- Your Strategy: Highlight a unique skill, like proficiency in a niche software, that sets you apart.

Analyzing your competition gives you a strategic edge.

Common Pitfalls in Competitive Analysis

1. Focusing Only on Competitors:

Don't lose sight of your own strengths and goals while analyzing others.

2. Underestimating Emerging Competitors:

Smaller or newer players can become serious threats over time.

3. Copying Competitors:

Success comes from differentiation, not imitation.

4. Overanalyzing:

Spending too much time on analysis can delay action.

Practical Tip: Use a SWOT Comparison

Create a SWOT chart comparing your strengths, weaknesses, opportunities, and threats against your competitors'. This highlights where you can excel.

Takeaway

Competitive Analysis helps you understand your rivals and find opportunities to stand out. By staying informed and adaptable, you can build strategies that set you apart.

Chapter 46: Red Teaming

What is Red Teaming?

Red Teaming is the practice of challenging your plans, strategies, or ideas by intentionally thinking like an opponent. It involves playing the role of a critic to uncover flaws, weaknesses, or risks that might otherwise be overlooked.

This model is used in military strategy, business planning, and decision-making to ensure ideas are well-prepared.

Why Red Teaming Matters

Without scrutiny, even the best plans can fail due to unforeseen issues. Red Teaming forces you to anticipate challenges and improve your ideas before implementing them.

For example:

- A company launching a product has a Red Team act as skeptical customers to identify potential problems, like unclear instructions or poor usability.

Example: Planning a New Budget

You're creating a personal budget to save money.

- Plan: Save 20% of your income monthly.

- Red Team Critique: What if unexpected expenses arise? Do you have a plan for emergencies?

- Revised Plan: Build an emergency fund alongside monthly savings.

Challenging your assumptions makes your plan more resilient.

How to Use Red Teaming

1. Assemble a Red Team:

Include people with different perspectives who can critique your plan objectively.

2. Identify Assumptions:

List the key assumptions your plan relies on.

3. Challenge the Plan:

Ask tough questions like What could go wrong? What would an opponent do?

4. Revise and Strengthen:

Use the feedback to address weaknesses and refine your plan.

Everyday Example of Red Teaming

Suppose you're preparing for a big presentation.

- Red Team: A friend pretends to be a skeptical audience, asking challenging questions.

- Outcome: You realize one slide is unclear and revise it for clarity.

This preparation ensures you're ready for real-world challenges.

Common Pitfalls in Red Teaming

1. Ignoring Feedback:

If you resist criticism, your plan won't improve.

2. Being Too Defensive:

Remember, critiques are meant to strengthen, not attack, your ideas.

3. Overcomplicating the Process:

Focus on major flaws, not minor details.

4. Failing to Involve Diverse Perspectives:

A homogeneous Red Team may miss critical blind spots.

Practical Tip: Roleplay Opposing Scenarios

When Red Teaming, imagine how a competitor or critic would approach your plan. This helps you anticipate challenges from different angles.

Takeaway

Red Teaming strengthens your plans by exposing weaknesses and testing assumptions. It's a powerful way to build resilience and confidence in your strategies.

Now, let's explore innovative tools for maximizing impact.

Chapter 47: Asymmetric Thinking

What is Asymmetric Thinking?

Asymmetric Thinking focuses on finding actions that require minimal effort but create maximum impact. Instead of working harder on everything, you look for leverage points — small changes or strategies that deliver outsized results.

This approach is about being efficient and strategic rather than expending effort evenly across all tasks.

Why Asymmetric Thinking Matters

Time and resources are limited. Asymmetric Thinking ensures you prioritize actions that create the most value, helping you achieve more with less.

For example:

- A small business focuses on a niche market instead of competing with larger companies, gaining loyal customers with less effort.

Example: Growing a Social Media Audience

You want to grow your social media following.

- Symmetric Approach: Post daily to all platforms with equal effort.

- Asymmetric Approach: Focus on one platform where your target audience is most active, creating tailored, high-quality content.

By concentrating on the highest-impact area, you grow faster and more effectively.

How to Apply Asymmetric Thinking

1. Identify Leverage Points:

Look for areas where small actions can create significant results.

2. Analyze the Effort-to-Impact Ratio:

Compare the resources required versus the potential outcome.

3. Focus on High-Impact Areas:

Prioritize tasks or strategies with the best return on investment.

4. Test and Adjust:

Experiment with different actions to find what works best.

Everyday Example of Asymmetric Thinking

Suppose you're trying to improve your health.

- Symmetric: Follow a strict workout routine and complex diet plan.

- Asymmetric: Start by improving sleep quality, which boosts energy and supports better decision-making for fitness and nutrition.

Focusing on one high-impact change simplifies the process and delivers better results.

Common Pitfalls in Asymmetric Thinking

1. Chasing Every Shortcut:

Not all "small actions" lead to big results. Focus on meaningful leverage points.

2. Overlooking Long-Term Effort:

Asymmetric Thinking is about smart effort, not avoiding effort entirely.

3. Ignoring Context:

What works in one situation might not apply elsewhere.

4. Underestimating Preparation:

Leveraging small actions often requires careful planning and insight.

Practical Tip: Ask, "What's My Biggest Lever?"

For any goal, identify the one action or strategy that could create the most significant result with minimal effort.

Takeaway

Asymmetric Thinking maximizes results by focusing on high-leverage actions. It's a mindset for achieving big goals efficiently and strategically.

Let's explore collaborative tools for gathering different perspectives.

Chapter 48: Crowdsourcing Ideas

What is Crowdsourcing Ideas?

Crowdsourcing Ideas involves gathering input, feedback, or solutions from a large group of people, often through open calls or collaborative platforms. It leverages the collective intelligence of a group to solve problems or generate creative ideas.

This approach works because diverse perspectives often lead to more innovative and well-rounded solutions.

Why Crowdsourcing Matters

Your own perspective is limited. Crowdsourcing taps into a wider range of experiences, skills, and insights, uncovering ideas you might not have considered.

For example:

- A company launching a product asks customers for feature suggestions, ensuring the product meets real needs.

Example: Planning a Community Event

You're organizing a neighborhood festival and unsure what activities to include.

- Crowdsourcing: Conduct a survey asking residents for their preferences. The responses help you prioritize activities that will attract the most participants.

How to Crowdsource Ideas

1. Define the Problem or Goal:

Clearly communicate what you're trying to solve or achieve.

2. Choose the Right Platform:

Use tools like surveys, social media, or brainstorming sessions to gather input.

3. Encourage Participation:

Make it easy for people to contribute and emphasize that their input is valued.

4. Analyze and Implement:

Sort through the ideas, identify patterns, and integrate the best ones into your plan.

Everyday Example of Crowdsourcing

Suppose you're redecorating your living room.

- Post options for paint colors on social media and ask friends for their opinions. Their feedback helps you choose a popular, appealing color.

Common Pitfalls in Crowdsourcing

1. Too Many Ideas:

Without clear criteria, sorting through responses can become overwhelming.

2. Ignoring Contributions:

Failing to act on ideas discourages future participation.

3. Overreliance on Popularity:

The most popular ideas aren't always the best—balance feedback with critical analysis.

4. Lack of Clarity:

Ambiguous requests lead to unfocused or irrelevant contributions.

Practical Tip: Use "Vote and Prioritize" Methods

After gathering ideas, let the group vote on the best options to narrow the focus efficiently.

Takeaway

Crowdsourcing Ideas taps into collective wisdom to solve problems and generate innovative solutions. By leveraging diverse input, you can achieve better outcomes collaboratively.

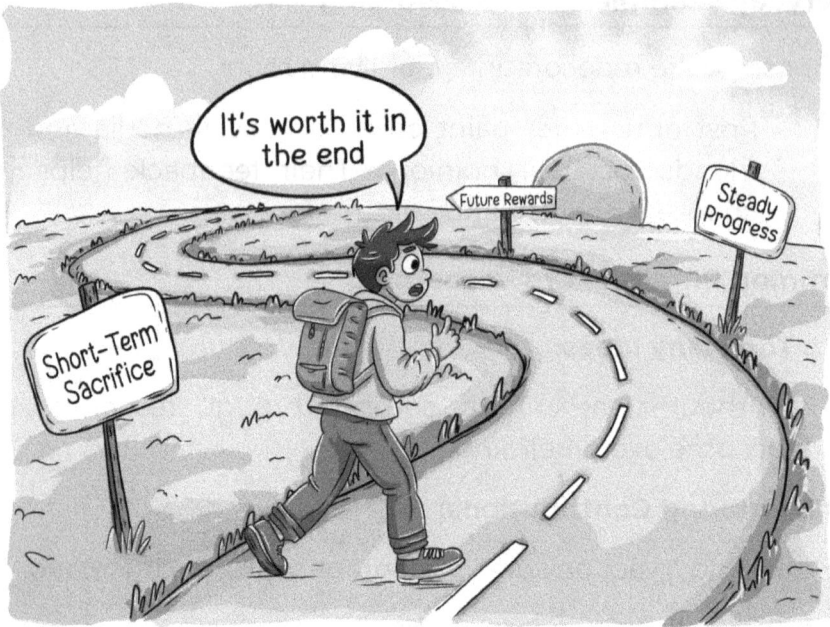

Chapter 49: Long-Term Thinking

What is Long-Term Thinking?

Long-Term Thinking focuses on making decisions today that benefit you in the future. It's about prioritizing sustainable progress and delayed gratification over short-term gains.

This model helps you achieve meaningful, lasting success by keeping your eyes on the big picture.

Why Long-Term Thinking Matters

Short-term decisions often feel rewarding but can derail your future goals. Long-Term Thinking ensures your actions align with what truly matters over time.

For example:

- Saving for retirement instead of spending on unnecessary luxuries ensures financial security in the future.

Example: Building a Fitness Routine

You want to get healthier.

- Short-Term Mindset: Do extreme workouts for quick results, risking burnout.

- Long-Term Mindset: Build sustainable habits like regular exercise and balanced nutrition, leading to lasting health improvements.

How to Practice Long-Term Thinking

1. Define Your Vision:

Identify your ultimate goals and what success looks like in the future.

2. Break Goals Into Steps:

Create smaller milestones that lead to the bigger picture.

3. Evaluate Decisions for Alignment:

Ask: Does this choice bring me closer to my long-term goals?

4. Be Patient:

Understand that meaningful results take time.

Everyday Example of Long-Term Thinking

Suppose you're tempted to buy an expensive gadget.

- Long-Term Thinking: Consider how saving that money could help you afford a bigger goal, like traveling or investing in your education.

Common Pitfalls in Long-Term Thinking

1. Overlooking Immediate Needs:

Balance long-term goals with current responsibilities.

2. Losing Focus:

Stay motivated by celebrating small wins along the way.

3. Underestimating Change:

Be flexible—adjust long-term plans as circumstances evolve.

4. Sacrificing Too Much:

Avoid burnout by allowing some short-term rewards along the journey.

Practical Tip: Use the "10/10/10 Rule"

For any decision, ask: *How will this affect me in 10 days? 10 months? 10 years?* This perspective highlights long-term impacts.

Takeaway

Long-Term Thinking helps you align your actions with lasting success. It's a strategy for building a meaningful future, one step at a time.

Let's move on to tools for handling uncertainty and unpredictability.

Chapter 50: Contingency Planning

What is Contingency Planning?

Contingency Planning involves preparing backup strategies in case your original plan doesn't work out. It's about expecting the unexpected and having a roadmap for navigating unforeseen challenges.

This model is essential for minimizing risks and staying adaptable under pressure.

Why Contingency Planning Matters

Life and projects rarely go exactly as planned. Without alternatives, setbacks can cause chaos. Contingency Planning ensures you can pivot quickly, reducing stress and keeping you on track.

For example:

- A company launching a product might prepare for supply chain delays by sourcing secondary suppliers in advance.

Example: Hosting an Outdoor Event

Suppose you're organizing a backyard party.

- **Plan A:** Clear skies and outdoor activities.

- **Contingency Plan:** Rent a tent and prepare indoor games in case it rains.

This backup ensures the party is successful, rain or shine.

How to Create a Contingency Plan

1. Identify Key Risks:

Consider what could go wrong and prioritize the most likely or impactful risks.

2. Develop Alternatives:

For each risk, outline specific actions you can take if it occurs.

3. Allocate Resources:

Ensure you have the tools, time, or budget needed to implement your backup plan.

4. Communicate the Plan:

Share your contingency strategies with relevant stakeholders.

Everyday Example of Contingency Planning

Imagine you're commuting to work.

- Plan A: Drive your usual route.

- Plan B: Check for traffic or public transport options in case of delays.

By preparing a backup, you ensure you arrive on time even if your primary route is blocked.

Common Pitfalls in Contingency Planning

1. Overlooking Low-Probability Risks:

Even unlikely events can have significant consequences. Prepare for them.

2. Failing to Test the Plan:

Backup plans should be reviewed and tested to ensure they're practical.

3. Ignoring Resources:

Contingency plans are useless if you lack the resources to execute them.

4. Relying Only on the Backup:

Don't neglect the original plan while focusing on contingencies.

Practical Tip: Use a "What If" Checklist

List potential scenarios starting with "What if ..." (e.g., *What if my flight is canceled?*). For each, write down a clear response.

Takeaway

Contingency Planning ensures you're ready for the unexpected. By preparing alternatives, you can face challenges calmly and confidently.

Communication Models

Chapter 51: The 5W Model

What is The 5W Model?

The 5W Model is a framework for gathering complete and clear information about any situation by asking five essential questions:

1. Who is involved?

2. What is happening?

3. Where is it occurring?

4. When did it or will it happen?

5. Why is it significant?

This model is used in journalism, problem-solving, and planning to ensure nothing important is overlooked.

Why The 5W Model Matters

Incomplete information leads to misunderstandings and poor decisions. The 5W Model organizes your thinking, ensuring all important aspects of a situation are addressed.

For example:

- A journalist covering a story ensures they answer all five questions to give readers a complete understanding.

Example: Planning a Business Meeting

Suppose you're organizing a team meeting.

- **Who:** Key team members.

- **What:** Discuss project deadlines.

- **Where:** Conference room or online.

- **When:** Thursday at 10 a.m.

- **Why:** To ensure everyone aligns on tasks.

Answering these questions ensures clarity and efficiency.

How to Use the 5W Model

1. Start with the Basics:

Use the 5Ws to outline the core details of any problem, plan, or project.

2. Expand Each Question:

Add context and specifics to each answer as needed.

3. Check for Gaps:

Review your answers to ensure nothing important is missing.

4. Communicate Clearly:

Use the 5Ws as a structure for presenting or explaining information.

Everyday Example of the 5W Model

Suppose you're planning a family trip.

- **Who:** Your family.
- **What:** A weekend getaway.
- **Where:** A nearby beach town.
- **When:** Next month.
- **Why:** To relax and spend quality time together.

The 5W Model ensures the trip is well-organized and everyone is on the same page.

Common Pitfalls in the 5W Model

1. Overlooking One W:

Skipping even one question can leave critical details unaddressed.

2. Being Too Vague:

Answers like "soon" or "someone" lack clarity. Be specific.

3. Overcomplicating Answers:

Keep answers focused and concise.

4. Failing to Adapt:

Adjust the 5Ws as new information emerges.

Practical Tip: Use the 5Ws for Problem-Solving

When facing a challenge, write down the 5Ws to clarify the situation and guide your response.

Takeaway

The 5W Model simplifies decision-making by organizing essential information into clear, actionable insights. It's a versatile tool for clarity and communication.

Now, let's explore models for enhancing understanding and collaboration.

Chapter 52: Active Listening

What is Active Listening?

Active Listening is the skill of fully concentrating on what someone is saying to understand their message completely. It involves more than just hearing words — it's about engaging with the speaker through attention, empathy, and feedback.

This model is essential for clear communication, strong relationships, and effective problem-solving.

Why Active Listening Matters

Many misunderstandings occur because people listen to respond, not to understand. Active Listening builds trust, reduces conflict, and ensures mutual understanding.

For example:

- A manager practicing Active Listening hears not only an employee's concerns but also the emotions behind them, leading to better solutions.

Example: Handling a Misunderstanding

Suppose a friend is upset about a canceled plan.

- Passive Listening: You nod while planning your response, missing their real frustration.

- Active Listening: You focus on their words, ask clarifying questions, and validate their feelings.

This approach resolves the issue more effectively.

How to Practice Active Listening

1. Give Full Attention:

Maintain eye contact and avoid distractions like phones or multitasking.

2. Show You're Listening:

Use nonverbal cues like nodding and facial expressions to signal engagement.

3. Ask Questions:

Clarify points with open-ended questions like *Can you tell me more about that?*

4. Paraphrase for Clarity:

Repeat back what you heard to confirm understanding (e.g., *So you're saying...*).

5. Avoid Interrupting:

Let the speaker finish before responding.

Everyday Example of Active Listening

Imagine your child is explaining their day at school.

- Active Listening: You listen without interrupting, ask questions about their favorite part, and summarize what they shared.

This builds connection and shows that their words matter.

Common Pitfalls in Active Listening

1. Getting Distracted:

Multitasking or letting your mind wander undermines the process.

2. Jumping to Solutions:

Sometimes, people just want to be heard, not "fixed."

3. Interrupting:

Cutting someone off discourages them from fully expressing their thoughts.

4. Ignoring Nonverbal Cues:

Pay attention to tone, body language, and emotions, not just words.

Practical Tip: Use the "Wait Rule"

Before responding, count to three silently. This ensures the speaker has finished and gives you time to formulate a thoughtful reply.

Takeaway

Active Listening strengthens communication by fostering understanding and trust. It's a simple yet powerful skill that improves every interaction.

Let's continue exploring tools for giving effective feedback.

Chapter 53: Feedback Framework

What is a Feedback Framework?

A Feedback Framework organizes constructive feedback into clear, actionable steps. It ensures feedback is specific, balanced, and focused on improvement rather than criticism.

This model is used in workplaces, education, and personal relationships to foster growth and understanding.

Why Feedback Frameworks Matter

Unstructured feedback often feels vague, harsh, or unhelpful. A framework ensures your message is clear, encouraging, and aligned with the recipient's goals.

For example:

- A manager uses a framework to praise an employee's strengths, highlight areas for improvement, and suggest specific next steps.

Example: Coaching a Team Member

Suppose a colleague struggles with time management.

- **What Went Well:** "You're thorough in completing tasks."

- **What Could Improve:** "Sometimes deadlines are missed due to detailed focus."

- **Suggestions for Growth:** "Try setting time limits for each task to stay on track."

This structure makes feedback constructive and actionable.

How to Use a Feedback Framework

1. Start Positive:

Highlight what the person is doing well to build confidence.

2. Be Specific About Improvements:

Focus on behaviors or actions, not personal traits (e.g., *"This report needs more detail"* instead of *"You're careless"*).

3. Provide Solutions:

Offer practical steps or tools to address the issue.

4. End on a Positive Note:

Reinforce your belief in the person's ability to improve.

Everyday Example of Feedback Framework

Imagine your child brings home a report card with mixed grades.

- "You've done a great job in math and science (What Went Well). Let's work on reading comprehension together (What Could Improve). Reading for 20 minutes daily could help (Suggestions for Growth)."

This feedback encourages them without feeling discouraging.

Common Pitfalls in Feedback Frameworks

1. Being Too Vague:

General comments like *"Good job"* don't provide actionable guidance.

2. Focusing Only on Negatives:

Balance constructive feedback with praise to maintain morale.

3. Overloading with Suggestions:

Stick to one or two key points for better focus.

4. Delivering Feedback Emotionally:

Keep your tone calm and professional to ensure the message is well-received.

Practical Tip: Use the "Feedback Sandwich"

Start with positive feedback, address the area for improvement, and end with encouragement.

Takeaway

A Feedback Framework turns criticism into constructive guidance, fostering growth and improvement. It's a valuable tool for building trust and achieving better results.

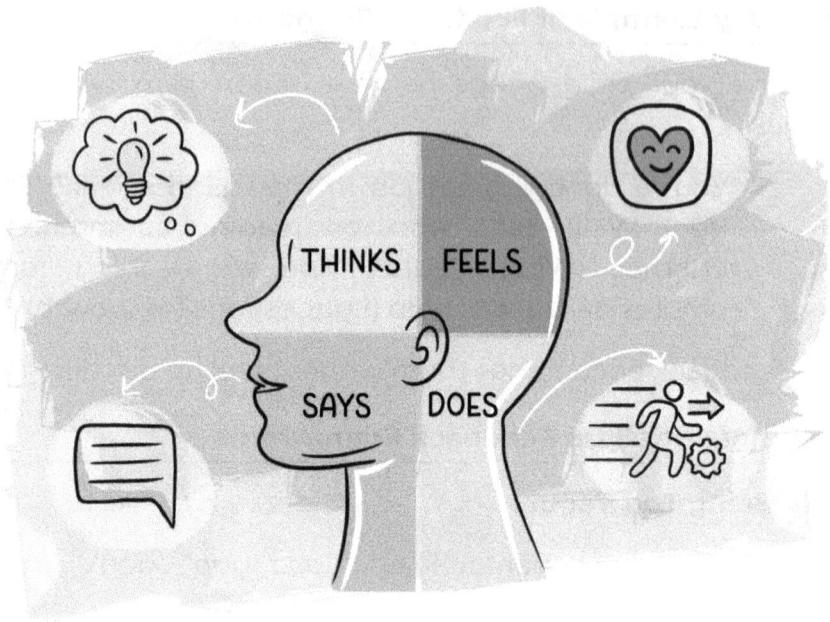

Chapter 54: Empathy Mapping

What is Empathy Mapping?

Empathy Mapping is a tool for understanding someone's experience by exploring what they say, think, feel, and do. It's used to gain deeper insights into their perspective, whether they're a customer, team member, or loved one.

This model helps you connect with others on a more meaningful level and design solutions that truly meet their needs.

Why Empathy Mapping Matters

Without empathy, solutions often miss the mark. Empathy Mapping uncovers hidden emotions, motivations, and concerns, ensuring your decisions are human-centered.

For example:

- A business designing a new app uses Empathy Mapping to understand users' frustrations with current solutions, creating features that address their pain points.

Example: Resolving a Customer Complaint

Suppose a customer complains about late delivery.

- **Says:** "This delay is unacceptable."

- **Thinks:** "They don't value my time."

- **Feels:** Frustrated and undervalued.

- **Does:** Writes a negative review.

Understanding these layers helps you respond with empathy, offering a sincere apology and proactive solution.

How to Create an Empathy Map

1. Define the Person:

Choose who you're mapping—customer, employee, or another individual.

2. Gather Data:

Use interviews, surveys, or observations to collect insights.

3. Fill the Sections:

Note what they:

- **Says:** Quotes or phrases they use.

- **Thinks:** Beliefs or motivations.

- **Feels:** Emotions driving their actions.

- **Does:** Observable behaviors.

4. Identify Patterns:

Look for connections between sections to better understand their experience.

Everyday Example of Empathy Mapping

Imagine helping a child with homework.

- **Says:** "This is too hard!"

- **Thinks:** "I'm not good at this subject."

- **Feels:** Frustrated and anxious.

- **Does:** Avoids the homework.

By empathizing, you offer encouragement and break the task into smaller, manageable steps.

Common Pitfalls in Empathy Mapping

1. Making Assumptions:

Base your map on real data, not guesses.

2. Overgeneralizing:

Avoid lumping people into overly broad categories. Focus on individual insights.

3. Ignoring Context:

A person's actions may depend on specific circumstances.

4. Focusing Only on Surface Behaviors:

Dive deeper to uncover underlying emotions and thoughts.

Practical Tip: Use Empathy Maps in Teams

When brainstorming, create an empathy map together to align perspectives and design better solutions.

Takeaway

Empathy Mapping deepens your understanding of others, leading to more meaningful connections and effective solutions.

Chapter 55: The Elevator Pitch

What is The Elevator Pitch?

An Elevator Pitch is a short, compelling statement that explains your idea, product, or value in the time it takes to ride an elevator (about 30 – 60 seconds).

This model ensures you can communicate your message clearly, concisely, and persuasively in any situation.

Why Elevator Pitches Matter

Opportunities often arise unexpectedly. Having a polished pitch ensures you can make a strong impression, whether networking, pitching an idea, or promoting your business.

For example:

- An entrepreneur meets an investor and delivers a brief but impactful pitch, sparking interest in their startup.

Example: Promoting a Freelance Business

Suppose you're a freelance graphic designer.

- Elevator Pitch: *"I help small businesses create eye-catching logos and branding that attract more customers. My designs have increased client engagement by 30%. I'd love to discuss how I can help your business stand out."*

This concise pitch highlights your value and invites further conversation.

How to Craft an Elevator Pitch

1. Identify Your Key Message:

Focus on what makes you or your idea unique and valuable.

2. Highlight the Benefits:

Explain how your audience will gain from what you're offering.

3. Keep It Simple:

Avoid jargon and stick to plain, engaging language.

4. End with a Call to Action:

Invite the listener to take the next step (e.g., schedule a meeting or ask questions).

Everyday Example of an Elevator Pitch

Suppose you're introducing yourself at a community event.

- Pitch: *"Hi, I'm Alex. I organize local clean-up projects to make our neighborhood greener and more enjoyable. We've already transformed two parks, and I'd love for you to join our next event!"*

This quick introduction communicates your mission and invites participation.

Common Pitfalls in Elevator Pitches

1. Rambling:

Keep your pitch concise and focused.

2. Being Too Generic:

Highlight what makes you unique.

3. Overloading with Details:

Focus on key points—leave room for follow-up questions.

4. Failing to Practice:

Rehearse until your pitch feels natural and confident.

Practical Tip: Use the "Who, What, Why" Formula

Include who you are, what you offer, and why it matters in your pitch.

Takeaway

An Elevator Pitch helps you communicate your value effectively in any situation. It's a powerful tool for making memorable first impressions.

Let's continue exploring tools for presenting ideas with clarity and structure.

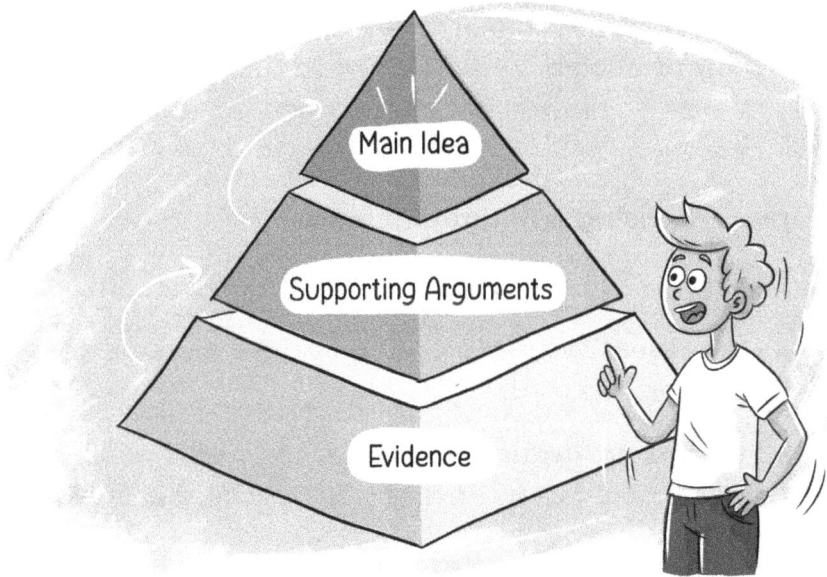

Chapter 56: The Pyramid Principle

What is The Pyramid Principle?

The Pyramid Principle is a communication model that organizes ideas from the top down: starting with the main conclusion, then explaining supporting arguments, and finally presenting detailed evidence.

This model ensures clarity and helps audiences understand and retain your message.

Why The Pyramid Principle Matters

Unstructured ideas confuse audiences. The Pyramid Principle organizes information logically, making complex topics clear and persuasive.

For example:

- A business executive uses the Pyramid Principle to present a plan to increase revenue, starting with the strategy, followed by specific actions and supporting data.

Example: Proposing a Budget Increase

Suppose you're requesting a higher project budget.

- **Main Idea:** We need a 20% budget increase to meet project goals.

- **Supporting Arguments:** Increased funding will ensure better tools, faster timelines, and higher quality.

- **Evidence:** Projects with similar budgets outperformed by 30%.

This structure makes your case compelling and easy to follow.

How to Use The Pyramid Principle

1. Start with the Conclusion:

Present your main idea or recommendation upfront.

2. Provide Supporting Arguments:

Explain why your conclusion is valid using 2–4 key points.

3. Back It Up with Evidence:

Offer data, examples, or research to reinforce each argument.

4. Keep It Logical:

Ensure the flow of ideas is clear and each layer builds on the one before.

Everyday Example of The Pyramid Principle

Suppose you're convincing a friend to take a weekend trip.

- **Main Idea:** Let's visit the beach this weekend.

- **Supporting Arguments:** It's relaxing, affordable, and close by.

- **Evidence:** The weather forecast is perfect, and gas prices are low.

This approach simplifies decision-making by presenting a clear case.

Common Pitfalls in The Pyramid Principle

1. Burying the Lead:

Don't save your main idea for last—state it upfront.

2. Overloading with Arguments:

Focus on a few strong points rather than overwhelming your audience.

3. Using Weak Evidence:

Ensure your data or examples are credible and relevant.

4. Ignoring Audience Needs:

Tailor your pyramid to address what matters most to your audience.

Practical Tip: Practice "Top-Down" Thinking

Before explaining a topic, write your main idea at the top, followed by 2–3 supporting points. Use this structure to guide your delivery.

Takeaway

The Pyramid Principle organizes your ideas for maximum clarity and impact. It's a powerful way to persuade, explain, and simplify complex topics.

Chapter 57: Storytelling

What is Storytelling?

Storytelling is the art of presenting information through narratives that engage emotions and imagination. It transforms data or ideas into memorable, relatable, and persuasive messages.

This model is widely used in marketing, leadership, and teaching to capture attention and inspire action.

Why Storytelling Matters

Facts alone often fail to inspire. Stories connect emotionally, making your message more impactful and easier to remember.

For example:

- A charity uses a personal story about someone they've helped to highlight the impact of donations, motivating more support.

Example: Motivating a Team

Suppose your team is behind schedule.

- Tell a story: *"Remember when we faced a similar deadline last year? By working together and staying focused, we not only met it but exceeded expectations. We can do that again now."*

This narrative inspires teamwork and confidence.

How to Use Storytelling

1. Start with a Hook:

Capture attention with a relatable situation, surprising fact, or question.

2. Present the Challenge:

Describe the problem or conflict, building tension and curiosity.

3. End with the Resolution:

Show how the challenge was overcome, leaving your audience inspired or informed.

4. Make It Personal:

Use real or relatable characters to make the story resonate.

Everyday Example of Storytelling

Imagine explaining a concept to a child.

- Instead of saying, *"Always tell the truth,"* share a story: *"Once, a boy lied about seeing a wolf. When a wolf really came, no one believed him."*

Stories make lessons memorable.

Common Pitfalls in Storytelling

1. Too Much Detail:

Keep your story concise and focused.

2. Forgetting the Audience:

Tailor your story to their interests and level of understanding.

3. Skipping the Resolution:

Without a satisfying ending, the story loses its impact.

4. Using Clichés:

Original, authentic stories resonate more than overused ones.

Practical Tip: Follow the "Hero's Journey"

Frame your story around a character facing a challenge, learning a lesson, and achieving a resolution.

Takeaway

Storytelling transforms your message into an engaging and memorable narrative. It's a timeless tool for inspiring action, understanding, and connection.

Let's continue exploring tools for refining clarity and enhancing communication.

Chapter 58: The 7 Cs of Communication

What are The 7 Cs of Communication?

The 7 Cs are principles for effective communication, ensuring your message is clear, complete, and well-received. They include:

1. Clear: Use simple, understandable language.

2. Concise: Avoid unnecessary words.

3. Concrete: Provide specific, tangible details.

4. Correct: Ensure accuracy in facts and grammar.

5. Coherent: Organize your message logically.

6. Complete: Cover all necessary points.

7. Courteous: Be respectful and considerate.

This model ensures your message resonates and achieves its purpose.

Why the 7 Cs Matter

Miscommunication leads to confusion and errors. The 7 Cs provide a framework for crafting messages that are precise, engaging, and effective.

For example:

- A leader delivering a company update ensures the message is clear, complete, and courteous to avoid misunderstandings and maintain morale.

Example: Writing an Email

Suppose you're inviting colleagues to a meeting.

- **Clear:** State the purpose of the meeting.

- **Concise:** Keep the email brief.

- **Concrete:** Include the date, time, and location.

- **Correct:** Double-check spelling and details.

- **Coherent:** Organize the email logically.

- **Complete:** Mention required materials.

- **Courteous:** Use a polite tone.

This ensures your email is effective and professional.

How to Apply the 7 Cs

1. Draft with Purpose:

Start by clarifying your goal and audience.

2. Review Each "C":

Evaluate your message against the 7 Cs checklist.

3. Edit for Simplicity:

Simplify language and remove unnecessary details.

4. Get Feedback:

Have someone review your message for clarity and tone.

Everyday Example of the 7 Cs

Imagine texting a friend about plans.

- Clear: *"Let's meet at the park."*

- Concise: *"2 PM, Saturday."*

- Concrete: *"By the fountain."*

Using the 7 Cs ensures nothing is missed.

Common Pitfalls in the 7 Cs

1. Overloading with Details:

Too much information dilutes the main point.

2. Using Jargon:

Avoid terms your audience may not understand.

3. Rushing the Process:

Skipping review risks errors or omissions.

4. Ignoring Tone:

Communication should be respectful and considerate.

Practical Tip: Create a Pre-Send Checklist

Before sending any message, quickly review it against the 7 Cs to ensure it's polished and effective.

Takeaway

The 7 Cs of Communication ensure your messages are clear, concise, and impactful. It's a versatile framework for improving understanding and engagement.

Change the frame, change the perspective

Chapter 59: Reframing

What is Reframing?

Reframing is the skill of changing the way you perceive a situation, problem, or challenge to see it in a new light. By shifting perspective, you can transform obstacles into opportunities or see setbacks as lessons.

This model is invaluable for problem-solving, emotional resilience, and creative thinking.

Why Reframing Matters

Humans naturally focus on problems or negative aspects of situations. Reframing helps you break out of this mindset, enabling more constructive, optimistic, and innovative thinking.

For example:

- A delayed flight can feel frustrating, but reframing it as an opportunity to relax and catch up on reading changes the emotional impact.

Example: Handling Criticism

Suppose you receive critical feedback on a project.

- Negative View: "They don't appreciate my work."

- Reframed View: "This is a chance to improve and grow my skills."

This new perspective motivates you to act positively instead of feeling discouraged.

How to Practice Reframing

1. Recognize Negative Thoughts:

Notice when you're stuck in a negative or unhelpful perspective.

2. Challenge Assumptions:

Ask: Is there another way to look at this? What am I overlooking?

3. Find the Opportunity:

Identify the potential benefits or lessons in the situation.

4. Reframe the Narrative:

Shift your focus to the positive or constructive aspects.

Everyday Example of Reframing

Imagine facing a tough workout.

- Initial Thought: "This is exhausting."

- Reframed Thought: "This challenge is making me stronger."

Reframing turns resistance into motivation.

Common Pitfalls in Reframing

1. Forcing Positivity:

Reframing isn't about ignoring reality. Balance optimism with practicality.

2. Ignoring the Lesson:

Focus on what you can learn, not just making yourself feel better.

3. Being Stuck in One View:

Explore multiple perspectives to find the most helpful one.

4. Using Vague Reframes:

Make your reframing specific and actionable.

Practical Tip: Use "What If" Questions

Ask yourself, *What if this situation were a hidden opportunity? What if this setback is setting me up for something better?*

Takeaway

Reframing shifts your perspective to unlock new possibilities and reduce negativity. It's a powerful tool for growth, resilience, and creative problem-solving.

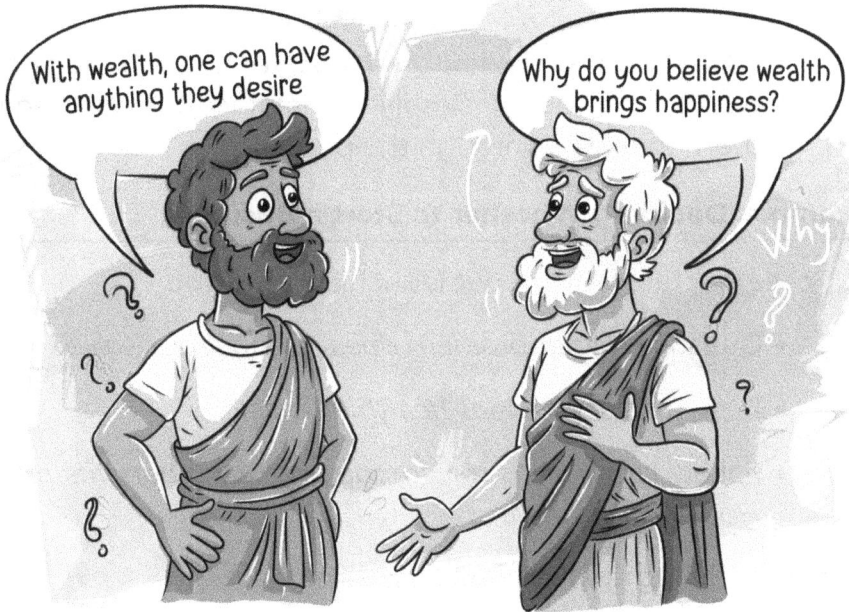

Chapter 60: The Socratic Method

What is The Socratic Method?

The Socratic Method is a dialogue-based approach to uncovering truth through questioning. Instead of giving answers, you ask thought-provoking questions to challenge assumptions, explore ideas, and arrive at deeper understanding.

This model is used in education, problem-solving, and decision-making to foster critical thinking.

Why the Socratic Method Matters

Humans often accept assumptions or surface-level explanations without question. The Socratic Method challenges you to think critically and dig deeper, leading to better decisions and insights.

For example:

- A teacher asks students *Why do you think this solution works?* instead of simply explaining it, encouraging them to reason through the problem.

Example: Deciding Whether to Start a Business

Suppose you're unsure about launching a startup.

- Question: *What problem does my business solve?*

- Response: *It provides healthier snacks.*

- Follow-Up: *Why is this important? Who benefits most? How will it stand out?*

This questioning clarifies your vision and strategy.

How to Use The Socratic Method

1. Start with a Broad Question:

Ask open-ended questions like *Why?* or *How?*

2. Follow the Answers:

Dive deeper into responses to uncover underlying assumptions or gaps.

3. Encourage Reflection:

Avoid giving answers; let the person arrive at conclusions through reasoning.

4. Challenge Contradictions:

Highlight inconsistencies to refine understanding.

Everyday Example of The Socratic Method

Imagine a friend is debating buying a car.

- You ask: *Why do you want this car? What's the benefit? Is it worth the cost?*

- This helps them consider their motivations and priorities before deciding.

Common Pitfalls in The Socratic Method

1. Being Confrontational:

Questions should guide, not intimidate or criticize.

2. Leading with Bias:

Avoid steering questions toward a specific answer.

3. Skipping Follow-Ups:

Surface-level answers often hide deeper insights—keep digging.

4. Overloading with Questions:

Focus on quality over quantity to avoid overwhelming the other person.

Practical Tip: Use "Why, What, How"

Start with *Why* to uncover purpose, move to *What* for specifics, and finish with *How* to explore solutions.

Takeaway

The Socratic Method fosters deeper understanding through thoughtful questioning. It's a versatile tool for clarifying ideas, solving problems, and inspiring critical thinking.

Behavioral and Cognitive Models

Chapter 61: Cognitive Bias Awareness

What is Cognitive Bias Awareness?

Cognitive Bias Awareness involves recognizing the mental shortcuts and errors in judgment that influence thinking. Biases, while sometimes helpful for quick decisions, often lead to flawed reasoning or assumptions.

This model is a foundational step for critical thinking and sound decision-making.

Why Cognitive Bias Awareness Matters

Biases shape your thoughts and actions, often without you realizing it. Awareness allows you to question assumptions, reduce errors, and make more rational choices.

For example:

- In hiring, someone aware of their biases ensures they assess candidates objectively, avoiding favoritism based on superficial factors.

Example: Buying a Car

Suppose you're influenced by flashy advertisements.

- Bias: You believe the advertised car is better, despite higher costs and fewer features.

- Awareness: You realize this bias and focus on comparing specs and reviews objectively.

This leads to a better, more informed purchase.

How to Recognize Cognitive Biases

1. Learn Common Biases:

Study biases like confirmation, anchoring, and availability to spot them in action.

2. Pause and Reflect:

Before making decisions, ask: Am I being influenced by assumptions or emotions?

3. Seek Diverse Perspectives:

Different viewpoints highlight blind spots and challenge your biases.

4. Practice Self-Awareness:

Regularly analyze your thinking patterns for signs of bias.

Everyday Example of Bias Awareness

Imagine you're debating switching careers.

- Bias: Overestimating risks due to fear of failure.

- Awareness: Questioning this fear helps you realize the benefits of the change outweigh the risks.

This clarity encourages confident decision-making.

Common Pitfalls in Bias Awareness

1. Assuming You're Unbiased:

Everyone has biases. Awareness is about managing, not eliminating, them.

2. Overcompensating:

Swinging too far in the opposite direction can create new biases.

3. Relying Solely on Awareness:

Awareness is the first step—take actions to mitigate biases.

4. Ignoring Feedback:

Feedback from others often reveals biases you miss.

Practical Tip: Use a Bias Checklist

Before decisions, run through common biases (e.g., *Am I favoring familiar ideas? Am I ignoring evidence that contradicts my beliefs?*).

Takeaway

Cognitive Bias Awareness helps you think more objectively by identifying and questioning mental shortcuts. It's the first step to clearer, more rational decisions.

Let's continue unpacking specific biases and how to counteract them.

Chapter 62: Anchoring Bias

What is Anchoring Bias?

Anchoring Bias occurs when initial information disproportionately influences decisions. Once an "anchor" is set, people tend to rely too heavily on it, even if it's irrelevant or misleading.

This model highlights the importance of questioning first impressions and reevaluating with fresh information.

Why Anchoring Bias Matters

Anchors can distort judgment, leading to suboptimal decisions. Recognizing this bias ensures you evaluate situations based on full context, not just the starting point.

For example:

- A store marks a $100 item as "50% off," making it feel like a great deal, even if $50 is still overpriced.

Example: Negotiating a Salary

Suppose a potential employer offers an initial salary of $50,000.

- With Bias: You focus on the anchor and negotiate only slightly higher.
- Without Bias: You research average salaries and confidently negotiate for $60,000, based on market data.

By resisting the anchor, you achieve better results.

How to Overcome Anchoring Bias

1. Delay Judgments:

Avoid making decisions immediately after encountering an anchor.

2. Gather Independent Data:

Look beyond the anchor for additional evidence or benchmarks.

3. Set Your Own Anchor:

Enter situations like negotiations with pre-established goals based on research.

4. Ask Critical Questions:

Challenge whether the initial information is relevant or reliable.

Everyday Example of Anchoring Bias

Imagine shopping for a TV.

- Anchor: A high-end model costs $2,000.

- Impact: A $1,200 TV seems affordable by comparison, even if it's more than you planned to spend.

Awareness of anchoring helps you reassess your actual needs and budget.

Common Pitfalls in Avoiding Anchoring

1. Ignoring Context:

Sometimes anchors are valuable starting points. Evaluate them carefully.

2. Rushing Decisions:

Quick decisions often reinforce the power of the anchor.

3. Underestimating Subtle Anchors:

Even casual comments or numbers can unconsciously influence thinking.

4. Overcorrecting:

Avoid dismissing all anchors—use them as one of many data points.

Practical Tip: Create Pre-Set Benchmarks

Before entering a decision, establish clear criteria or goals. This prevents reliance on external anchors.

Takeaway

Anchoring Bias reminds you to question the influence of initial information. By challenging anchors, you ensure decisions are grounded in context and data.

Chapter 63: Confirmation Bias

What is Confirmation Bias?

Confirmation Bias is the tendency to seek, interpret, and favor information that supports your existing beliefs while ignoring or dismissing evidence that challenges them.

This bias narrows your perspective, making it harder to see the full picture or change your mind.

Why Confirmation Bias Matters

When you only focus on confirming your beliefs, you miss opportunities to learn, improve, or make better decisions. Challenging this bias ensures you base conclusions on evidence, not assumptions.

For example:

- A person believing a specific diet works might only read success stories while ignoring studies showing mixed results.

Example: Debating a Purchase

Suppose you're considering buying a car.

- With Bias: You focus on reviews praising the car and ignore negative feedback.

- Without Bias: You weigh all reviews, both positive and negative, before deciding.

Considering all perspectives leads to a better-informed choice.

How to Overcome Confirmation Bias

1. Seek Opposing Views:

Actively look for evidence that contradicts your beliefs.

2. Ask Neutral Questions:

Frame inquiries to explore all possibilities, not just confirm your assumptions.

3. Evaluate All Evidence Equally:

Avoid dismissing information simply because it challenges your viewpoint.

4. Encourage Feedback:

Share your ideas with others and invite critical perspectives.

Everyday Example of Confirmation Bias

Imagine you believe one exercise is the best for fitness.

- With Bias: You only follow articles praising that exercise.

- Without Bias: You explore different methods, discovering complementary workouts for better results.

Awareness of this bias broadens your understanding.

Common Pitfalls in Addressing Confirmation Bias

1. Avoiding Discomfort:

Challenging beliefs can feel uncomfortable but is necessary for growth.

2. Overvaluing Familiar Sources:

Prioritize credible evidence over sources you already trust.

3. Cherry-Picking Data:

Avoid selecting only evidence that aligns with your views.

4. Overcorrecting:

Balance challenging your beliefs with maintaining a critical eye on new evidence.

Practical Tip: Use the "Devil's Advocate" Approach

Regularly challenge your ideas by asking, *What if I'm wrong? What would disprove this belief?*

Takeaway

Confirmation Bias reminds us to question our assumptions and seek balanced perspectives. Confronting this bias leads to more informed, open-minded decision-making.

Let's continue exploring how recent experiences can distort judgment.

Chapter 64: Availability Heuristic

What is the Availability Heuristic?

The Availability Heuristic is a mental shortcut where you base decisions on information that comes to mind quickly — often recent or emotionally vivid experiences — rather than on all relevant data.

This heuristic helps with quick thinking but often leads to biased judgments.

Why the Availability Heuristic Matters

Relying solely on recent or memorable events skews decisions, ignoring broader patterns or probabilities. Recognizing this heuristic helps you think more critically and holistically.

For example:

- After hearing about a plane crash, someone may overestimate the risk of flying, despite data showing it's safer than driving.

Example: Estimating Health Risks

Suppose a friend mentions getting sick after eating sushi.

- With Heuristic: You avoid sushi, believing it's unsafe.
- Without Heuristic: You consider food safety statistics, realizing sushi is generally low-risk.

Critical evaluation ensures balanced decisions.

How to Avoid the Availability Heuristic

1. Pause Before Judging:

Ask: Am I relying on a recent or dramatic event rather than overall evidence?

2. Look at the Bigger Picture:

Research statistics or trends to gain a broader understanding.

3. Recognize Emotional Influence:

Be aware of how vivid or emotional events may cloud objectivity.

4. Compare Multiple Sources:

Seek diverse perspectives to counterbalance single, memorable instances.

Everyday Example of the Availability Heuristic

Imagine you're planning a trip and recall a recent storm at your destination.

- Heuristic: You cancel the trip, assuming bad weather is likely.
- Balanced View: You check the forecast, finding clear skies ahead.

This approach separates emotions from facts.

Common Pitfalls in the Availability Heuristic

1. Overvaluing Recent Events:

Fresh memories feel more relevant but aren't always representative.

2. Ignoring Probabilities:

Uncommon events can feel more frequent due to emotional impact.

3. Relying on Anecdotes:

Individual stories rarely reflect broader trends.

4. Resisting Data:

Vivid events can feel more "real" than abstract statistics.

Practical Tip: Use Data for Context
When making decisions, ask: *What do the numbers say? Are there broader patterns I'm overlooking?*

Takeaway
The Availability Heuristic shows the importance of balancing vivid memories with objective data. By questioning first impressions, you make more rational, informed decisions.

Let's continue exploring how social dynamics shape behavior.

Chapter 65: Social Proof

What is Social Proof?

Social Proof is the tendency to imitate others' actions or beliefs, assuming their choices are correct. It's a psychological shortcut: if many people are doing something, it must be the right thing to do.

This model explains phenomena like trends, herd behavior, and peer pressure.

Why Social Proof Matters

While Social Proof can be helpful for quick decisions, it often leads to blindly following the crowd without questioning its wisdom. Recognizing this influence helps you act intentionally rather than reactively.

For example:

- You might buy a product with thousands of 5-star reviews, assuming it's superior without checking if the reviews are genuine.

Example: Choosing a Restaurant

Suppose you're deciding where to eat.

- With Social Proof: You pick the restaurant with a long line, assuming it's better.

- With Awareness: You consider reviews, menu options, and your preferences, making a more thoughtful choice.

Balancing social cues with independent judgment leads to better decisions.

How to Use or Avoid Social Proof

1. Recognize Its Influence:

Notice when you're making choices based on others' behavior.

2. Evaluate the Crowd's Expertise:

Ask: Are these people informed or just following each other?

3. Combine Social Proof with Research:

Use others' actions as a starting point but verify with data or personal needs.

4. Lead When Needed:

Don't hesitate to go against the crowd when your judgment suggests otherwise.

Everyday Example of Social Proof

Imagine everyone at work is using a specific app for productivity.

- With Awareness: You evaluate whether the app aligns with your workflow before adopting it.

This prevents wasting time on tools that may not suit your needs.

Common Pitfalls in Social Proof

1. Blind Conformity:

Following others without questioning their reasons can lead to poor decisions.

2. Assuming Popular Equals Good:

Popularity often reflects marketing, not quality.

3. Ignoring Personal Needs:

What works for others may not work for you.

4. Overreliance on Trends:

Trends often fade, leaving you with outdated choices.

Practical Tip: Ask, "Why Is Everyone Doing This?"

Consider whether the crowd's actions are based on wisdom or simply herd mentality.

Takeaway

Social Proof highlights the power of group influence on decisions. Balancing social cues with critical thinking ensures your choices align with your goals.

Let's continue exploring how habits shape behavior over time.

Chapter 66: Habit Formation

What is Habit Formation?

Habit Formation is the process of developing behaviors through repetition and reinforcement. Habits consist of three parts:

1. **Cue:** A trigger for the habit.

2. **Routine:** The action or behavior itself.

3. **Reward:** The benefit or satisfaction you gain from the behavior.

By understanding this cycle, you can build positive habits or replace negative ones.

Why Habit Formation Matters

Habits shape daily life and long-term outcomes. Good habits compound over time, leading to personal growth and success, while bad habits hold you back.

For example:

- A daily habit of reading improves knowledge, while a habit of procrastination stalls progress.

Example: Building a Morning Routine

Suppose you want to exercise each morning.

- Cue: Set out workout clothes the night before.
- Routine: Go for a 20-minute jog.
- Reward: Enjoy the post-exercise energy boost.

Repeating this loop solidifies the habit.

How to Form New Habits

1. Start Small:

Focus on manageable changes to build consistency.

2. Tie Habits to Cues:

Link new habits to existing routines (e.g., floss after brushing your teeth).

3. Reward Yourself:

Reinforce habits with immediate, meaningful rewards.

4. Be Patient:

Habits take time to stick—progress is gradual.

Everyday Example of Habit Formation

Imagine wanting to drink more water daily.

- Cue: Keep a water bottle on your desk.

- Routine: Take a sip every time you check your phone.

- Reward: Feel refreshed and hydrated.

These small steps make the habit effortless over time.

Common Pitfalls in Habit Formation

1. Setting Unrealistic Goals:

Overambitious habits are harder to maintain.

2. Skipping Rewards:

Without rewards, habits feel like chores.

3. Relying on Willpower Alone:

Environmental cues and systems are more effective.

4. Giving Up After Slip-Ups:

Missing a day doesn't mean failure—just restart.

Practical Tip: Use "Habit Stacking"

Attach new habits to existing ones, like meditating after your morning coffee, to integrate them seamlessly.

Takeaway

Habit Formation creates lasting change through small, consistent actions. Understanding the habit loop empowers you to build behaviors that support your goals.

Let's now look how triggers shape behavior and decision-making.

Chapter 67: Pavlovian Conditioning

What is Pavlovian Conditioning?

Pavlovian Conditioning, also known as classical conditioning, is the process of associating a neutral stimulus (like a sound) with a specific response due to repeated pairings. Over time, the neutral stimulus triggers the response automatically.

This model, discovered by Ivan Pavlov, explains many learned behaviors in both animals and humans.

Why Pavlovian Conditioning Matters

Understanding conditioning helps you recognize how external triggers influence behavior, often subconsciously. With awareness, you can shape or break conditioned responses.

For example:

- A phone notification sound triggers an automatic urge to check your phone, even if the message isn't urgent.

Example: Eating Habits

Suppose you snack every time you watch TV.

- Cue: Turning on the TV.

- Response: Feeling the urge to grab a snack.

- Awareness: Recognizing the pattern lets you replace the habit with drinking water instead.

How to Recognize and Influence Conditioning

1. Identify the Cue:

Notice the stimulus that triggers your response.

2. Examine the Response:

Reflect on whether the reaction serves your goals or needs.

3. Replace or Reinforce Behavior:

Pair the cue with a new response (e.g., exercising when stressed instead of overeating).

4. Practice Consistency:

Repeatedly pair the new behavior with the cue to recondition your response.

Everyday Example of Pavlovian Conditioning

Imagine you associate the sound of your alarm with dread.

- Solution: Replace your alarm tone with a favorite song to create a more positive morning experience.

This reconditions your emotional response to the cue.

Common Pitfalls in Pavlovian Conditioning

1. Ignoring Negative Cues:

Many unhelpful habits stem from unnoticed triggers.

2. Overgeneralizing Responses:

Conditioned responses may spread to similar cues. Recognize and address this.

3. Relying on Willpower Alone:

Changing conditioned responses requires restructuring, not just resisting.

4. Inconsistency:

Inconsistent pairing weakens new associations.

Practical Tip: Use Positive Triggers

Intentionally pair cues (like setting a calming ringtone) with positive actions to create healthier habits.

Takeaway

Pavlovian Conditioning highlights the power of cues in shaping behavior. By identifying and reshaping triggers, you can condition responses that align with your goals.

Let's continue exploring strategies for managing emotions effectively.

Chapter 68: Emotional Regulation

What is Emotional Regulation?

Emotional Regulation is the ability to manage and control emotional reactions, especially in stressful or challenging situations. It involves recognizing emotions, understanding their causes, and choosing constructive responses.

This model is essential for maintaining mental health, strong relationships, and effective decision-making.

Why Emotional Regulation Matters

Unregulated emotions often lead to impulsive actions, poor decisions, or conflict. By managing emotions, you stay composed, think clearly, and respond effectively.

For example:

- Instead of snapping during an argument, emotional regulation helps you pause, reflect, and communicate calmly.

Example: Handling Workplace Stress

Suppose a project deadline gets moved up unexpectedly.

- Without Regulation: Panic leads to hasty decisions and frustration with teammates.

- With Regulation: You pause, prioritize tasks, and ask for support, maintaining focus and efficiency.

How to Practice Emotional Regulation

1. Recognize Emotions Early:

Identify feelings as they arise before they escalate.

2. Pause Before Reacting:

Take a deep breath or count to ten to gain perspective.

3. Reframe the Situation:

Shift your perspective to see challenges as opportunities or lessons.

4. Choose Constructive Responses:

Respond in ways that align with your goals and values.

Everyday Example of Emotional Regulation

Imagine getting cut off in traffic.

- Initial Reaction: Anger and frustration.

- Regulated Response: You remind yourself it's not personal, take a deep breath, and continue driving safely.

This approach keeps emotions from escalating.

Common Pitfalls in Emotional Regulation

1. Suppressing Emotions:

Ignoring feelings can lead to long-term stress or burnout.

2. Overreacting:

Small triggers shouldn't derail your composure.

3. Blaming Others:

Focus on controlling your response rather than external factors.

4. Skipping Reflection:

Failing to analyze emotional patterns limits growth.

Practical Tip: Practice Mindfulness

Regular mindfulness exercises help you stay aware of emotions and manage them calmly.

Takeaway

Emotional Regulation empowers you to respond thoughtfully instead of reacting impulsively. It's a vital tool for navigating life's ups and downs with clarity and composure.

Now, let's look at how expectations influence outcomes.

Chapter 69: Self-Fulfilling Prophecy

What is a Self-Fulfilling Prophecy?

A Self-Fulfilling Prophecy occurs when your expectations about a situation influence your behavior, causing the expected outcome to materialize. Positive beliefs lead to success, while negative ones often create failure.

This model demonstrates the power of mindset in shaping reality.

Why Self-Fulfilling Prophecies Matter

Your beliefs shape your actions, which in turn affect outcomes. Being aware of this cycle helps you challenge negative expectations and cultivate confidence.

For example:

- A student who believes they'll fail a test might study less, reinforcing the belief and leading to poor performance.

Example: Preparing for a Job Interview

Suppose you expect to perform well in an interview.

- With Positive Beliefs: Confidence leads you to prepare thoroughly and present yourself effectively.

- With Negative Beliefs: Doubts make you nervous and unprepared, resulting in a weaker performance.

Your mindset determines how you act, influencing the outcome.

How to Break Negative Prophecies

1. Recognize Limiting Beliefs:

Identify negative thoughts or assumptions holding you back.

2. Reframe Expectations:

Replace self-defeating beliefs with empowering ones, like *I can improve with effort.*

3. Act on Positive Beliefs:

Behave in ways that align with your new, constructive mindset.

4. Celebrate Small Wins:

Reinforce positive beliefs by acknowledging progress.

Everyday Example of a Self-Fulfilling Prophecy

Imagine you assume a colleague doesn't like you.

- Negative Belief: You avoid them, creating awkwardness that confirms your assumption.

- Positive Belief: You greet them warmly, fostering a friendly relationship instead.

Your actions can either escalate or dissolve tension.

Common Pitfalls in Self-Fulfilling Prophecies

1. Clinging to Negative Assumptions:

Doubts often feel valid but are worth questioning.

2. Ignoring Behavior Patterns:

Focusing solely on outcomes neglects the actions driving them.

3. Overgeneralizing Past Failures:

Previous results don't dictate future possibilities.

4. Resisting Change:

Breaking negative cycles requires consistent effort and patience.

Practical Tip: Use Affirmations

Practice daily affirmations like *I am capable of handling challenges* to build positive expectations.

Takeaway

The Self-Fulfilling Prophecy highlights how beliefs shape actions and outcomes. By fostering positive expectations, you create a cycle of growth and success.

Chapter 70: Grit and Resilience

What are Grit and Resilience?

Grit is the passion and perseverance to pursue long-term goals, while resilience is the ability to recover quickly from setbacks. Together, they empower you to stay focused and overcome challenges, no matter how tough the journey.

These traits are essential for sustained success and personal growth.

Why Grit and Resilience Matter

Life's challenges often derail progress. Grit keeps you moving forward, while resilience helps you bounce back stronger. Together, they build the mental endurance needed to achieve meaningful goals.

For example:

- An athlete training for a marathon relies on grit to stick to their plan and resilience to recover from injuries or missed milestones.

Example: Starting a Business

Suppose your first product launch fails.

- Without Grit: You feel defeated and give up.

- With Grit: You analyze what went wrong, improve the product, and try again.

This persistence eventually leads to success.

How to Cultivate Grit and Resilience

1. Set Meaningful Goals:

Pursue objectives that truly inspire and motivate you.

2. Embrace Setbacks as Lessons:

View failures as opportunities to learn and grow.

3. Build a Support System:

Surround yourself with people who encourage and inspire you.

4. Practice Self-Compassion:

Treat yourself kindly during tough times to maintain focus and energy.

Everyday Example of Grit and Resilience

Imagine learning a new skill, like cooking.

- With Grit: You keep practicing despite initial failures.

- With Resilience: Burned meals or mistakes don't discourage you.

Over time, persistence transforms you into a confident chef.

Common Pitfalls in Building Grit and Resilience

1. Focusing Only on Motivation:

Discipline sustains effort when motivation fades.

2. Expecting Instant Results:

Grit requires patience—progress is often slow but steady.

3. Avoiding Discomfort:

Growth happens when you face challenges head-on.

4. Ignoring Rest:

Resilience depends on balancing effort with recovery.

Practical Tip: Use the "10-Year Vision"

Imagine where you want to be in 10 years. Use this vision to fuel your grit and remind yourself why perseverance is worth it.

Takeaway

Grit and resilience help you navigate setbacks and stay committed to long-term goals. Together, they form the foundation for enduring success and growth.

Let's now delve into financial and economic models that guide decision-making.

Financial and Economic Models

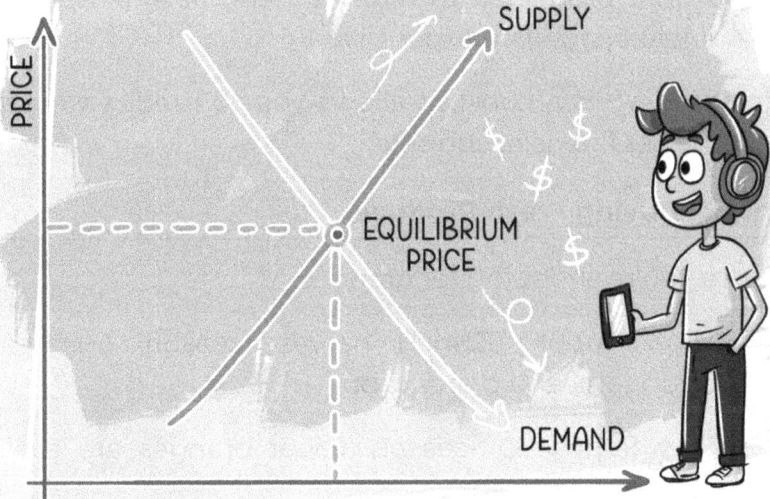

Chapter 71: Supply and Demand

What is Supply and Demand?

Supply and Demand is a fundamental economic model that explains how prices are determined in a market.

- **Supply:** How much of a product or service is available.

- **Demand:** How much people want it.

- The price adjusts to balance supply and demand, reaching the equilibrium where they meet.

Why Supply and Demand Matter

This model helps you understand why prices fluctuate and how to make decisions based on market conditions.

For example:

- A rare product with high demand (like limited-edition sneakers) will be expensive.

Understanding this concept allows you to predict trends and make smarter financial choices.

Example: Buying Fresh Produce

Suppose you're shopping for oranges.

- High Supply: During harvest season, oranges are abundant, and prices drop.

- Low Supply: Off-season, fewer oranges are available, and prices rise.

Knowing this, you can plan to buy in-season for better value.

How to Apply Supply and Demand

1. Monitor Market Trends:

Notice how availability and popularity affect prices.

2. Time Your Decisions:

Buy when supply is high, and demand is low to get the best deals.

3. Consider Alternatives:

When demand drives prices up, explore substitutes (e.g., apples instead of oranges).

4. Evaluate Future Value:

Anticipate shifts in supply or demand to make informed investments.

Everyday Example of Supply and Demand

Imagine concert tickets for a popular band.

- Limited supply and high demand cause ticket prices to surge.

- If you act early or choose less popular seats, you save money.

This understanding helps you optimize your spending.

Common Pitfalls in Supply and Demand

1. Ignoring Market Signals:

Prices often reflect changes in supply or demand—pay attention to these signals.

2. Acting Reactively:

Waiting too long during high demand can lead to missed opportunities or higher costs.

3. Assuming Trends Are Permanent:

Market conditions fluctuate—don't expect high demand to last forever.

4. Focusing Only on Price:

Quality and availability also affect value.

Practical Tip: Use Price Tracking Tools

Apps or websites that monitor price trends help you buy when supply and demand are most favorable.

Takeaway

Supply and Demand explain market behaviors, helping you navigate prices and make strategic choices.

Let's continue exploring how psychological traps can distort financial decisions.

Chapter 72: Sunk Cost Fallacy

What is the Sunk Cost Fallacy?

The Sunk Cost Fallacy occurs when you continue investing time, money, or effort into something simply because you've already spent resources on it—even if it's no longer worth pursuing.

It's a psychological trap that keeps you stuck in unproductive situations.

Why the Sunk Cost Fallacy Matters

Clinging to sunk costs leads to poor decisions and wasted resources. Recognizing this fallacy helps you cut losses and focus on better opportunities.

For example:

- Staying in an unfulfilling job because you've spent years in the field, despite better prospects elsewhere.

Example: Watching a Bad Movie

Suppose you've paid for a ticket to a movie you're not enjoying.

- With the Fallacy: You stay because you've already spent money.

- Without the Fallacy: You leave and spend your time on something more fulfilling.

Letting go of sunk costs improves overall satisfaction.

How to Avoid the Sunk Cost Fallacy

1. Focus on Future Value:

Ask: Does continuing add value moving forward?

2. Ignore Past Investments:

Treat previous costs as irrelevant—they can't be recovered.

3. Make Rational Assessments:

Evaluate situations based on current and future benefits, not past commitments.

4. Set Clear Exit Strategies:

Decide in advance when you'll walk away if results don't meet expectations.

Everyday Example of the Sunk Cost Fallacy

Imagine you're halfway through a book you don't enjoy.

- Fallacy: You finish it because you've already invested time.

- Rational Choice: You stop reading and start a book that excites you.

This frees your time for more rewarding activities.

Common Pitfalls in Avoiding the Sunk Cost Fallacy

1. Emotional Attachment:

Sentimental value can make it harder to let go.

2. Fear of Regret:

Worrying about "wasted" resources keeps you stuck.

3. External Pressure:

Others may encourage sticking with sunk costs due to shared investments.

4. Overthinking Losses:

Focusing too much on past losses distracts from future gains.

Practical Tip: Ask, "What Would I Do If I Started Fresh?"

This question shifts your focus to current value rather than past costs.

Takeaway

The Sunk Cost Fallacy teaches you to prioritize future value over past investments. Letting go of unproductive commitments opens the door to better opportunities.

Chapter 73: Scarcity Principle

What is the Scarcity Principle?

The Scarcity Principle suggests that limited availability increases an item's perceived value. When something is rare or hard to obtain, it feels more desirable.

This principle is often used in marketing, but it also influences personal decision-making, creating urgency where it might not be necessary.

Why the Scarcity Principle Matters

Scarcity can cloud judgment, leading you to make impulsive or emotional decisions. Recognizing this principle helps you evaluate opportunities more rationally.

For example:

- A "limited-time offer" can pressure you to buy something you don't really need.

Example: Buying Event Tickets

Suppose you see a notice: *"Only 5 tickets left!"*

- With Scarcity Bias: You rush to purchase without thinking.

- Without Scarcity Bias: You pause to assess if you actually want to attend.

Being aware of scarcity marketing ensures thoughtful choices.

How to Avoid Scarcity Traps

1. Pause and Reflect:

Ask: Would I want this if it weren't limited?

2. Evaluate True Value:

Focus on an item's actual utility or benefits rather than its rarity.

3. Avoid Emotional Decisions:

Take a moment to detach emotionally before acting.

4. Question Marketing Tactics:

Recognize when scarcity is manufactured to create pressure.

Everyday Example of the Scarcity Principle

Imagine a sale on gadgets that says, "Offer ends tonight!"

- With Awareness: You evaluate whether the gadget is useful, ignoring the urgency.

- Without Awareness: You buy impulsively and later regret the purchase.

This approach ensures rational spending.

Common Pitfalls in the Scarcity Principle

1. FOMO (Fear of Missing Out):

Scarcity triggers FOMO, making you feel irrational urgency.

2. Overvaluing Rare Items:

Limited availability doesn't always equal higher quality.

3. Underestimating Abundance:

Common items are often just as valuable but overlooked.

4. Succumbing to Pressure:

High-pressure tactics exploit emotional responses.

Practical Tip: Use the "Wait Rule"

Before acting on scarcity, wait 24 hours. If it still feels important after the pause, proceed thoughtfully.

Takeaway

The Scarcity Principle shows how limited availability can skew perception and decision-making. Awareness helps you act based on true value, not artificial urgency.

Let's continue exploring how to balance risks and rewards effectively.

Chapter 74: Risk-Reward Ratio

What is the Risk-Reward Ratio?

The Risk-Reward Ratio is a tool for evaluating whether a potential reward justifies the risk involved. It helps you decide if the upside of an opportunity outweighs the possible downsides.

This model is used in investing, business, and personal decisions to find the right balance.

Why the Risk-Reward Ratio Matters

Risk is unavoidable, but not all risks are worth taking. Understanding this ratio ensures your decisions are strategic rather than reckless.

For example:

- Investing in a startup with high growth potential might bring huge rewards, but the risk of failure is significant.

Example: Deciding on a Career Change

Suppose you're considering leaving your job for a new opportunity.

- Risks: Uncertainty, lower initial salary.
- Rewards: Higher long-term growth, alignment with your goals.

If the rewards outweigh the risks, the decision is worth pursuing.

How to Use the Risk-Reward Ratio

1. Identify Risks:

List potential downsides of the decision.

2. Evaluate Rewards:

Consider short- and long-term benefits.

3. Compare Magnitudes:

Assess if the potential gain justifies the possible loss.

4. Prepare Mitigation Plans:

Develop strategies to minimize risks while pursuing rewards.

Everyday Example of the Risk-Reward Ratio

Imagine buying a used car at a low price.

- Risks: Repairs might be costly.

- Rewards: Significant savings if the car is reliable.

Weighing these factors helps you make an informed purchase.

Common Pitfalls in Risk-Reward Analysis

1. Underestimating Risks:

Optimism can blind you to potential downsides.

2. Overvaluing Rewards:

Big rewards might distract from low probabilities of success.

3. Ignoring Mitigation:

Many risks can be reduced with planning.

4. Paralysis by Analysis:

Overthinking risks can prevent action altogether.

Practical Tip: Assign Probabilities

Estimate the likelihood of success and failure for a clearer picture of the ratio.

Takeaway

The Risk-Reward Ratio helps you make balanced decisions by weighing potential outcomes thoughtfully.

Let's look at a further way that you can improve productivity and resource allocation.

Chapter 75: The Law of Diminishing Returns

What is The Law of Diminishing Returns?

The Law of Diminishing Returns states that as you invest more effort, resources, or time into something, the added benefits decrease after a certain point.

This concept applies to productivity, spending, and resource allocation.

Why The Law of Diminishing Returns Matters

More effort doesn't always equal more results. Recognizing when returns diminish helps you allocate resources efficiently.

For example:

- Spending hours editing a project may improve it initially, but over-editing can waste time with little added benefit.

Example: Studying for an Exam

Suppose you study for 8 hours straight.

- Initial Hours: Significant learning and retention.

- Later Hours: Fatigue reduces focus, and retention drops.

Knowing when to take breaks maximizes efficiency.

How to Apply the Law of Diminishing Returns

1. Set Limits:

Define how much time or effort is reasonable for a task.

2. Monitor Progress:

Track results to see when additional effort brings diminishing returns.

3. Balance Quality and Efficiency:

Aim for "good enough" rather than perfection when returns taper off.

4. Reallocate Resources:

Shift time and energy to areas with higher potential impact.

Everyday Example of Diminishing Returns

Imagine working overtime to earn more money.

- Early Hours: Significant financial benefit.

- Excess Hours: Fatigue reduces productivity and work quality.

Recognizing the tipping point prevents burnout.

Common Pitfalls in Diminishing Returns

1. Chasing Perfection:

Excessive effort on small details often wastes time.

2. Ignoring Costs:

Additional input may cost more than the benefit it provides.

3. Overestimating Capacity:

Exhaustion limits how much value you can add.

4. Failing to Reassess:

Regularly evaluate whether continued effort is worth it.

Practical Tip: Use Time Caps

Set time limits for tasks to maintain productivity and avoid diminishing returns.

Takeaway

The Law of Diminishing Returns reminds you to work smarter, not harder, by recognizing when additional effort no longer adds value.

Now, let's continue by reviewing financial models for assessing value.

Chapter 76: ROI
(Return on Investment)

What is ROI (Return on Investment)?

ROI measures the profitability of an investment by comparing the net return to the initial cost. It's a simple formula:

net income ÷ cost of investment × 100

This model helps you evaluate whether an investment (time, money, or resources) is worth it.

Why ROI Matters

Every decision involves trade-offs. ROI ensures you allocate resources to opportunities that deliver the best results.

For example:

- Investing $1,000 in marketing that generates $2,000 in sales delivers a 100% ROI, doubling your money.

Example: Deciding on a Training Program

Suppose you're considering a $500 course to improve skills that might lead to a promotion.

- ROI: If the promotion increases your income by $2,000 annually, the ROI is (2000 500)/500×100=300%.$(2000 - 500) / 500 \times 100 = 300\%$.(2000 500)/500×100=300%.

Evaluating ROI helps you decide whether the investment is worthwhile.

How to Use ROI

1. Calculate Net Return:

Subtract the cost from the total benefit.

2. Compare Alternatives:

Analyze ROI across multiple options to prioritize the best one.

3. Factor in Intangible Benefits:

Consider qualitative outcomes like skill growth or reputation, even if they're hard to quantify.

4. Monitor Progress:

Reassess ROI periodically to ensure continued value.

Everyday Example of ROI

Imagine buying a $50 monthly gym membership.

- High ROI: You use the gym regularly and improve your health.

- Low ROI: You rarely go, wasting money.

Assessing ROI motivates better resource use.

Common Pitfalls in ROI Analysis

1. Ignoring Long-Term Returns:

Some benefits, like education, take time to materialize.

2. Overlooking Hidden Costs:

Include all expenses, like maintenance or time investment.

3. Focusing Only on Money:

ROI isn't always financial—it can include personal or professional growth.

4. Relying on Assumptions:

Base calculations on realistic data, not overly optimistic projections.

Practical Tip: Use an ROI Calculator

Online tools simplify ROI calculations, helping you compare options quickly and accurately.

Takeaway

ROI helps you make smarter decisions by quantifying the value of investments. Prioritizing high-ROI opportunities leads to better outcomes.

SMART USE OF RESOURCES

Big Goal

Chapter 77: Leverage

What is Leverage?

Leverage is the strategic use of resources — money, tools, skills, or time — to amplify results with less effort. It's about working smarter, not harder, by multiplying the impact of your actions.

For example:

- Borrowing money to invest in a profitable business is financial leverage.

Why Leverage Matters

Without leverage, progress is slow and effort-intensive. Effective leverage accelerates growth and maximizes potential.

For example:

- An entrepreneur delegates routine tasks to focus on business strategy, multiplying their impact.

Example: Using Financial Leverage

Suppose you invest $20,000 in a property by borrowing $80,000.

- With Leverage: If the property's value increases by 10% ($10,000), your return is 50% on your $20,000.

- Without Leverage: Investing only $20,000 delivers just a 10% return ($2,000).

Leverage amplifies the outcome, but it also increases risk if returns don't materialize.

How to Use Leverage Wisely

1. Identify High-Impact Areas:

Focus resources where they'll create the greatest return.

2. Start Small:

Test leverage strategies on manageable projects before scaling.

3. Balance Risk and Reward:

Ensure potential gains outweigh risks.

4. Monitor Performance:

Regularly evaluate whether leverage is delivering the expected results.

Everyday Example of Leverage

Imagine automating bill payments.

- Without Leverage: You manually pay each bill monthly.

- With Leverage: Automation saves time and reduces errors, allowing focus on more important tasks.

Small leverage points create big efficiency gains.

Common Pitfalls in Leverage

1. Overleveraging:

Taking on excessive risk can lead to losses if things don't go as planned.

2. Misallocating Resources:

Focus leverage where it provides the highest returns.

3. Neglecting Monitoring:

Unchecked leverage can lead to inefficiencies or financial strain.

4. Underestimating Costs:

Consider hidden expenses, like interest or maintenance.

Practical Tip: Use the "80/20 Rule"

Leverage resources to focus on the 20% of actions that generate 80% of results.

Takeaway

Leverage multiplies results by amplifying your resources strategically. Using it wisely accelerates success while managing risks.

Let's continue exploring

the importance of financial timing.

Today's Dollar   Future Value

Chapter 78: The Time Value of Money (TVM)

What is the Time Value of Money?

The Time Value of Money (TVM) states that a dollar today is worth more than a dollar in the future because it can be invested to grow. This model emphasizes the power of compounding and the cost of delaying financial decisions.

For example:

- Investing $1,000 at a 5% annual return grows to $1,276 in 5 years, demonstrating how money increases over time.

Why the Time Value of Money Matters

Understanding TVM helps you prioritize early investment and

minimize unnecessary delays in financial planning.

For example:

- Saving for retirement early allows compounding to work its magic, reducing the total amount you need to save later.

Example: Delaying Loan Payments

Suppose you have the option to defer a $5,000 loan payment for one year.

- With TVM: Investing $5,000 now at 10% returns $500 in one year, covering part of the loan cost.

- Without TVM: Deferring the payment saves nothing, losing the opportunity to grow your money.

TVM helps you decide whether deferral benefits you financially.

How to Apply the Time Value of Money

1. Invest Early:

Start saving or investing as soon as possible to maximize compounding.

2. Minimize Idle Money:

Ensure your money is actively working for you through investments or savings accounts.

3. Factor in Inflation:

Remember that money loses purchasing power over time due to inflation.

4. Use TVM Calculations:

Tools like future value or present value formulas help you evaluate financial decisions.

Everyday Example of TVM

Imagine you receive $1,000 and consider saving it under your mattress versus investing it.

- With TVM: Investing grows the $1,000 over time, while saving it under the mattress loses value due to inflation.

This awareness motivates better financial decisions.

Common Pitfalls in TVM

1. Procrastinating on Investments:

Delaying reduces the power of compounding.

2. Overlooking Inflation:

Inflation erodes the value of stagnant money.

3. Ignoring Opportunity Costs:

Leaving money idle sacrifices potential gains.

4. Misjudging Risk:

Seek balanced returns that align with your financial goals.

Practical Tip: Use Compound Interest Calculators

These tools show how small investments today grow significantly over time, reinforcing the importance of early action.

Takeaway

The Time Value of Money highlights the importance of acting early and investing wisely. It's a foundational concept for building long-term wealth.

Let's continue exploring financial efficiency.

Chapter 79: Arbitrage

What is Arbitrage?

Arbitrage is the process of taking advantage of price differences for the same item in different markets to earn a profit. It's a risk-free way to capitalize on inefficiencies in pricing.

For example:

- Buying stocks at a lower price in one market and selling them at a higher price in another.

Why Arbitrage Matters

Arbitrage reveals opportunities to maximize gains with minimal risk. It's commonly used in finance but also applies to everyday situations like flipping items or currency exchange.

For example:

- A traveler exchanges currency at a low rate in one city and sells it for a higher rate in another.

Example: Reselling Products

Suppose you notice a popular gadget is cheaper online than in local stores.

- With Arbitrage: You buy it online and resell it locally at a profit.

- Without Arbitrage: You miss the chance to profit from the price difference.

Arbitrage allows you to turn market inefficiencies into opportunities.

How to Spot Arbitrage Opportunities

1. Compare Prices Across Markets:

Look for differences in prices between locations, platforms, or vendors.

2. Act Quickly:

Arbitrage opportunities are often short-lived as markets adjust.

3. Factor in Costs:

Include transaction fees, shipping, or taxes to calculate net profit.

4. Use Technology:

Tools like price comparison apps or financial platforms make identifying arbitrage easier.

Everyday Example of Arbitrage

Imagine buying bulk concert tickets at an early-bird discount.

- Arbitrage: Sell the tickets closer to the event when demand drives prices up.

This simple practice turns timing and price gaps into profit.

Common Pitfalls in Arbitrage

1. Overlooking Hidden Costs:

Fees or taxes can eat into profits.

2. Timing Issues:

Prices can change before you act, erasing the opportunity.

3. Overestimating Demand:

Ensure there's a buyer for what you're reselling.

4. Legal Risks:

Some forms of arbitrage may violate rules or regulations.

Practical Tip: Start Small

Begin with low-cost arbitrage opportunities, like reselling discounted items, to build confidence and refine your skills.

Takeaway

Arbitrage transforms price differences into profit by identifying and acting on inefficiencies. It's a sharp tool for making the most of market opportunities.

Let's continue exploring how to do smarter financial planning.

We need to set aside more for emergencies—remember last month's car repairs?

Good point. Let's adjust the budget and forecast how much we can save for unexpected expenses going forward.

Chapter 80: Budgeting and Forecasting

What is Budgeting and Forecasting?

Budgeting involves creating a detailed plan for how you'll spend or allocate money, while forecasting predicts future financial outcomes based on current trends. Together, they ensure you stay on track and prepare for the unexpected.

For example:

- A household budget helps you control monthly spending, while forecasting projects how much you'll save over a year.

Why Budgeting and Forecasting Matter

Without budgeting, spending can spiral out of control. Forecasting helps you anticipate challenges and seize opportunities, ensuring financial stability and growth.

For example:

- A company uses forecasting to predict revenue, enabling smarter investments and hiring decisions.

Example: Planning a Vacation

Suppose you're saving for a trip.

- Budget: Allocate $2,000 for flights, lodging, and food.

- Forecast: Predict how much you'll save monthly to reach your goal in 6 months.

This approach ensures you stay within budget and meet your timeline.

How to Create a Budget and Forecast

1. List Income and Expenses:

Break down all sources of income and fixed or variable expenses.

2. Set Financial Goals:

Decide priorities, like paying off debt, saving for emergencies, or investing.

3. Track Spending:

Use apps or spreadsheets to monitor expenses and stay within limits.

4. Adjust Forecasts Regularly:

Update projections as your income or expenses change.

Everyday Example of Budgeting

Imagine you want to reduce dining out expenses.

- Budget: Limit dining to $100 per month.

- Forecast: Calculate how much this change saves over a year and redirect it toward other goals.

This plan turns small changes into significant financial improvements.

Common Pitfalls in Budgeting and Forecasting

1. Being Too Optimistic:

Overestimating income or underestimating expenses creates unrealistic plans.

2. Ignoring Emergencies:

Failing to account for unexpected costs can derail budgets.

3. Lack of Consistency:

Sporadic tracking undermines the accuracy of forecasts.

4. Not Reviewing Goals:

Financial priorities evolve—review budgets regularly to stay aligned.

Practical Tip: Use the 50/30/20 Rule

Allocate 50% of income to needs, 30% to wants, and 20% to savings or debt repayment.

Takeaway

Budgeting and Forecasting provide a clear financial roadmap, helping you achieve goals and prepare for the future.

Let's now shift to leadership and influence models to explore strategies for guiding and inspiring others.

Leadership and Influence Models

Chapter 81: Servant Leadership

What is Servant Leadership?

Servant Leadership is a leadership style where the leader prioritizes the needs of their team, empowering them to grow and succeed. Instead of focusing on personal authority, servant leaders emphasize collaboration, empathy, and service.

This approach builds trust, loyalty, and strong relationships, making teams more effective and motivated.

Why Servant Leadership Matters

Traditional "command and control" leadership often limits team potential. Servant Leadership creates an environment where people thrive, fostering creativity, productivity, and engagement.

For example:

- A manager who asks, *How can I support you?* encourages employees to solve problems confidently, knowing they have the leader's backing.

Example: Supporting Team Growth

Suppose a team member struggles with a project.

- Command Leadership: Criticize their performance and demand improvement.

- Servant Leadership: Provide resources, coaching, and encouragement to help them succeed.

This approach builds trust and develops skills.

How to Practice Servant Leadership

1. Prioritize Listening:

Understand your team's needs, concerns, and goals.

2. Empower Others:

Delegate responsibilities, allowing team members to take ownership.

3. Focus on Development:

Invest in training, mentorship, and growth opportunities.

4. Lead by Example:

Model the values and behaviors you expect from your team.

Everyday Example of Servant Leadership

Imagine leading a volunteer group for a charity event.

- Servant Leadership: Ensure everyone understands their role, offer support, and personally handle overlooked tasks.

This ensures the event runs smoothly while strengthening the team dynamic.

Common Pitfalls in Servant Leadership

1. Overextending Yourself:

Balancing team needs with personal responsibilities is crucial.

2. Avoiding Tough Decisions:

Being supportive doesn't mean avoiding accountability or challenges.

3. Neglecting Strategic Vision:

Focus on individual growth while keeping the team aligned with larger goals.

4. Mistaking Service for Weakness:

Servant Leadership requires strength and confidence, not submission.

Practical Tip: Conduct Regular Check-Ins

Ask team members what they need to succeed and how you can help, reinforcing a culture of support.

Takeaway

Servant Leadership transforms teams by focusing on empowerment and collaboration. It's a leadership style rooted in service, trust, and shared success.

Let's continue exploring leadership models.

Chapter 82: Transactional vs. Transformational Leadership

What is Transactional vs. Transformational Leadership?

Transactional Leadership focuses on structured goals, rewards, and responsibilities. It emphasizes maintaining order and efficiency.

Transformational Leadership inspires innovation and change by motivating teams to pursue a shared vision beyond their immediate tasks.

Both approaches are valuable, depending on the situation.

Why These Leadership Styles Matter

Understanding when to use each style improves your ability to lead effectively:

- **Transactional Leadership:** Best for predictable, task-oriented environments (e.g., meeting deadlines).

- **Transformational Leadership:** Ideal for inspiring creativity and adapting to change (e.g., launching a new project).

For example:

- A factory manager uses transactional leadership to ensure safety protocols are followed, while a tech startup CEO adopts transformational leadership to innovate products.

Example: Leading a Team Through Change

Suppose you're implementing new software.

- Transactional Leadership: Provide clear instructions, deadlines, and training resources.

- Transformational Leadership: Explain how the software will improve workflows and inspire enthusiasm for the change.

Blending both styles ensures smooth adoption and long-term motivation.

How to Balance Both Styles

1. Understand the Context:

Use transactional methods for structure and transformational methods for vision.

2. Communicate Clearly:

Set clear expectations while inspiring creativity and ownership.

3. Reward Achievements:

Recognize both routine successes and innovative contributions.

4. Adapt as Needed:

Shift between styles based on team needs and goals.

Everyday Example of Blending Leadership Styles

Imagine organizing a school fundraiser.

- Transactional: Assign tasks, set deadlines, and track progress.
- Transformational: Motivate volunteers by sharing the positive impact their efforts will have on the community.

This approach ensures efficiency and enthusiasm.

Common Pitfalls in Leadership Styles

1. Being Too Rigid:

Over-relying on one style limits effectiveness.

2. Neglecting Structure:

Transformational leaders must ensure practical execution.

3. Overlooking Motivation:

Transactional leaders should consider team morale and engagement.

4. Failing to Adapt:

Leadership needs change depending on challenges and goals.

Practical Tip: Use Transformational Leadership to Set the Vision

Then, apply Transactional Leadership to execute it efficiently.

Takeaway

Transactional and Transformational Leadership complement each other. Knowing when to use each style builds balanced, dynamic teams.

Let's continue exploring leadership strategies that prevent stagnation and build emotional intelligence.

Chapter 83: The Peter Principle

What is The Peter Principle?

The Peter Principle states that people in hierarchical organizations are often promoted until they reach their "level of incompetence." This means they are advanced to roles they're unprepared for, leading to decreased effectiveness.

This concept emphasizes the importance of skill alignment in career growth.

Why The Peter Principle Matters

Promotions based solely on past performance can place people in positions they can't handle, harming both the individual and the organization. Recognizing this risk ensures better role fit and sustainable success.

For example:

- A great salesperson may be promoted to a managerial role but struggle due to a lack of leadership skills.

Example: Avoiding Misaligned Promotions

Suppose an employee excels in a technical role.

- Without Awareness: They're promoted to management without assessing leadership aptitude.
- With Awareness: They're given leadership training or a role aligned with their strengths.

Proper alignment maximizes their impact and satisfaction.

How to Prevent The Peter Principle

1. Assess Skills Before Promoting:

Ensure candidates have the skills needed for the new role.

2. Provide Training:

Equip employees with the tools to succeed in higher positions.

3. Consider Lateral Moves:

Recognize that growth isn't always vertical; lateral roles can enhance expertise.

4. Evaluate Performance Continuously:

Monitor effectiveness in new roles and offer support as needed.

Everyday Example of The Peter Principle

Imagine a teacher promoted to principal due to classroom

success.

- Risk: Administrative duties require different skills, leading to struggles.

- Solution: Train them in leadership and management before the promotion.

This approach ensures smooth transitions.

Common Pitfalls in The Peter Principle

1. Ignoring Skill Gaps:

Past success doesn't guarantee future competence.

2. Overpromoting Out of Loyalty:

Promotions should be based on readiness, not tenure or relationships.

3. Underestimating Training Needs:

Assume every promotion requires a learning curve.

4. Avoiding Difficult Conversations:

Address mismatches promptly to prevent long-term harm.

Practical Tip: Use Competency Assessments

Evaluate readiness for promotion with tools that assess skills, leadership potential, and adaptability.

Takeaway

The Peter Principle highlights the risks of promoting without preparation. Aligning roles with skills ensures growth benefits both individuals and organizations.

EMPATHY

LOGIC

Chapter 84: Emotional Intelligence

What is Emotional Intelligence?

Emotional Intelligence (EI) is the ability to understand, manage, and influence emotions — both your own and others'. It involves five key components:

1. **Self-Awareness:** Recognizing your emotions.

2. **Self-Regulation:** Managing emotional responses.

3. **Motivation:** Staying focused and positive.

4. **Empathy:** Understanding others' feelings.

5. **Social Skills:** Building relationships and managing conflicts.

Why Emotional Intelligence Matters

While technical skills are vital, EI determines how effectively you collaborate, lead, and navigate challenges. High EI fosters trust, resilience, and teamwork.

For example:

- A leader with strong EI diffuses tensions during a heated meeting, maintaining productivity and morale.

Example: Handling Workplace Conflict

Suppose two colleagues disagree on a project.

- Without EI: Escalating emotions lead to unresolved conflict.

- With EI: A leader listens empathetically, validates concerns, and guides the team to a constructive resolution.

This approach ensures harmony and progress.

How to Develop Emotional Intelligence

1. Practice Self-Reflection:

Regularly analyze your emotional responses and their triggers.

2. Improve Empathy:

Listen actively and consider others' perspectives before reacting.

3. Strengthen Communication:

Use clear, respectful language to express needs and resolve misunderstandings.

4. Respond, Don't React:

Take a moment to process emotions before acting.

Everyday Example of Emotional Intelligence

Imagine a friend shares their frustration about work.

- With EI: You listen attentively, empathize, and offer supportive feedback.

This deepens trust and strengthens the relationship.

Common Pitfalls in Emotional Intelligence

1. Overemphasizing Empathy:

Balancing empathy with practicality prevents emotional burnout.

2. Ignoring Boundaries:

High EI doesn't mean tolerating harmful behavior.

3. Focusing Only on Others:

Managing your emotions is as crucial as understanding others'.

4. Underestimating Complexity:

EI requires ongoing practice and adaptability.

Practical Tip: Use the "Pause and Reflect" Method

When emotions run high, pause for a moment to reflect on your feelings and goals before responding.

Takeaway

Emotional Intelligence enhances decision-making, relationships, and leadership. Cultivating EI creates stronger teams and more meaningful interactions.

Chapter 85: Influence Strategies

What are Influence Strategies?

Influence strategies are techniques used to guide others' decisions, actions, or opinions while fostering collaboration and mutual respect. Effective influence is built on trust, understanding, and clear communication — not manipulation.

These strategies are essential for leadership, negotiation, and building strong relationships.

Why Influence Strategies Matter

Influence helps you align diverse perspectives and motivate action without coercion. Whether persuading a client or rallying a team, effective strategies ensure collaboration and success.

For example:

- A project manager uses influence to secure buy-in for a new process by showing its benefits to the team.

Example: Gaining Support for a New Initiative

Suppose you propose automating a manual workflow.

- Without Strategy: Resistance arises due to unclear benefits.

- With Strategy: You explain how automation saves time, offer examples of success, and address concerns.

This builds trust and encourages adoption.

How to Apply Influence Strategies

1. Build Rapport:

Establish trust by understanding others' needs and values.

2. Use Logic and Emotion:

Combine data with relatable stories to appeal to both reason and feelings.

3. Leverage Reciprocity:

Offer help or value first to create goodwill and mutual cooperation.

4. Be Consistent:

Align your actions with your words to maintain credibility.

5. Involve Others:

Encourage input and collaboration to foster ownership of decisions.

Everyday Example of Influence

Imagine convincing your family to adopt a healthier lifestyle.

- Influence Strategy: Share personal benefits, suggest easy changes, and involve them in planning meals or activities.

This approach inspires collective effort toward the goal.

Common Pitfalls in Influence Strategies

1. Overusing Authority:

Influence relies on respect, not forcing compliance.

2. Neglecting Empathy:

Understanding others' perspectives is key to meaningful persuasion.

3. Focusing Solely on Benefits:

Address concerns to build trust and overcome resistance.

4. Appearing Insincere:

Authenticity strengthens influence; manipulation erodes it.

Practical Tip: Use the "WIIFM" Principle

Frame your message around *What's In It For Me* from the other person's perspective to make it compelling.

Takeaway

Influence strategies empower you to align goals, inspire action, and build strong relationships. Practicing these techniques fosters collaboration and long-term success.

Let's explore further how it is possible to productively strengthens teams and relationships.

Chapter 86: Conflict Resolution

What is Conflict Resolution?

Conflict Resolution is the process of addressing disagreements constructively to find mutually acceptable solutions. It involves open communication, empathy, and a focus on shared goals rather than individual differences.

This model strengthens relationships, promotes collaboration, and minimizes disruptions.

Why Conflict Resolution Matters

Unresolved conflicts create tension, reduce productivity, and damage trust. Effective resolution fosters understanding, innovation, and teamwork.

For example:

- Two colleagues disagree on a project's direction. Conflict resolution helps them align their perspectives and work toward a shared goal.

Example: Resolving Workplace Disputes

Suppose a team member feels excluded from decisions.

- Without Resolution: Frustration grows, harming morale.

- With Resolution: Open dialogue addresses their concerns, clarifies roles, and restores harmony.

This process strengthens collaboration and trust.

How to Resolve Conflicts Effectively

1. Stay Calm:

Approach the situation with a clear mind and balanced emotions.

2. Listen Actively:

Understand all perspectives without interrupting or judging.

3. Focus on Interests, Not Positions:

Address underlying needs rather than surface-level demands.

4. Explore Win-Win Solutions:

Seek outcomes that satisfy all parties whenever possible.

5. Set Ground Rules:

Establish respectful communication to keep discussions productive.

Everyday Example of Conflict Resolution

Imagine a disagreement with a roommate about shared expenses.

- Without Resolution: Arguments create tension.
- With Resolution: You discuss openly, agree on a fair split, and set clear boundaries.

This approach strengthens understanding and avoids future issues.

Common Pitfalls in Conflict Resolution

1. Avoiding the Issue:

Ignoring conflicts only worsens them over time.

2. Becoming Defensive:

Focus on solutions rather than assigning blame.

3. Overlooking Emotional Impact:

Address feelings as well as facts to fully resolve the conflict.

4. Rushing the Process:

Allow time for thoughtful discussion and mutual agreement.

Practical Tip: Use "I" Statements

Express your feelings without blaming others (e.g., *I feel concerned about deadlines* instead of *You're always late*).

Takeaway

Conflict Resolution transforms disagreements into opportunities for growth and collaboration. It's an essential skill for fostering harmony and achieving shared goals.

Let's continue with practical strategies for effective leadership and management.

Chapter 87: Delegation

What is Delegation?

Delegation is the process of assigning tasks or responsibilities to others based on their skills and expertise. It's not about offloading work but empowering team members to contribute meaningfully while freeing up the leader to focus on strategic priorities.

Why Delegation Matters

Effective delegation maximizes efficiency, develops team capabilities, and prevents burnout for leaders. It's essential for balancing workload and achieving ambitious goals.

For example:

- A manager delegates data analysis to a skilled team member, allowing them to focus on client presentations.

Example: Organizing an Event

Suppose you're leading a charity fundraiser.

- Without Delegation: You handle logistics, promotion, and budgeting, risking overwhelm and mistakes.

- With Delegation: Assign tasks based on strengths (e.g., a marketer handles promotion, a detail-oriented member manages logistics).

This approach ensures smoother execution and team ownership.

How to Delegate Effectively

1. Match Tasks to Skills:

Assign responsibilities to individuals best suited for the job.

2. Define Clear Expectations:

Explain objectives, timelines, and desired outcomes.

3. Provide Resources and Support:

Equip team members with the tools and guidance they need to succeed.

4. Trust and Empower:

Avoid micromanaging—give team members autonomy to perform their tasks.

5. Follow Up Regularly:

Monitor progress and provide feedback without hovering.

Everyday Example of Delegation

Imagine planning a family reunion.

- Effective Delegation: Assign cooking, venue setup, and activity planning to different family members, focusing on coordination yourself.

This reduces stress and ensures everyone contributes.

Common Pitfalls in Delegation

1. Delegating Without Clarity:

Ambiguity leads to confusion and errors.

2. Micromanaging:

Constant oversight undermines trust and autonomy.

3. Overloading High Performers:

Distribute tasks evenly to avoid burnout among capable team members.

4. Failing to Provide Support:

Lack of resources or guidance can hinder performance.

Practical Tip: Use the "80% Rule"

If someone can perform a task 80% as well as you, delegate it. Their skills will improve with practice.

Takeaway

Delegation fosters collaboration, efficiency, and growth by leveraging the strengths of the entire team. It's a key skill for achieving both individual and collective success.

Let's now explore adaptability in leadership.

Chapter 88: Situational Leadership

What is Situational Leadership?

Situational Leadership is a flexible leadership approach that adapts to the needs, skills, and motivation levels of team members. Leaders shift between four styles:

1. **Directing:** Providing clear instructions and close supervision.

2. **Coaching:** Guiding and encouraging while involving the team in decision-making.

3. **Supporting:** Offering support and autonomy for experienced individuals.

4. **Delegating:** Assigning responsibility to highly skilled, self-reliant team members.

Why Situational Leadership Matters

No single leadership style fits every scenario. Adaptability ensures you provide the right level of guidance and support to maximize team effectiveness.

For example:

- A new hire may need detailed instructions (Directing), while a senior team member thrives with minimal oversight (Delegating).

Example: Managing a New Team

Suppose you're leading a team with varying experience levels.

- New Members: Use Directing to help them understand processes.
- Experienced Members: Use Delegating to let them lead initiatives.

Adapting your approach builds confidence and optimizes team contributions.

How to Practice Situational Leadership

1. Assess Each Individual:

Evaluate team members' competence and commitment for specific tasks.

2. Match Style to Needs:

Choose the leadership style that best supports their current abilities.

3. Communicate Clearly:

Ensure team members understand your expectations and their responsibilities.

4. Monitor Progress:

Adjust your approach as team members grow and circumstances change.

Everyday Example of Situational Leadership

Imagine coaching a youth sports team.

- Beginners: Use Directing to teach basics.
- Advanced Players: Shift to Supporting or Delegating, allowing them to take initiative.

This flexibility helps everyone perform at their best.

Common Pitfalls in Situational Leadership

1. Using One-Size-Fits-All Styles:

Tailor your approach to each individual's needs.

2. Failing to Reassess:

Team members' needs evolve—adjust your style accordingly.

3. Overcomplicating Decisions:

Keep adjustments simple and intuitive.

4. Ignoring Team Feedback:

Collaboration improves alignment and effectiveness.

Practical Tip: Use the "GROW" Model

Guide conversations with team members by discussing their **Goals**, **Reality**, **Options**, and **Way Forward.**

Takeaway

Situational Leadership optimizes outcomes by adapting your style to team members' unique needs. It's a dynamic approach that fosters growth and resilience.

Let's explore ways to strengthens group collaboration and success.

Chapter 89: Team Dynamics

What are Team Dynamics?

Team Dynamics describe the interpersonal relationships, roles, and behaviors within a group that influence its performance and cohesion. Positive dynamics drive collaboration and productivity, while negative dynamics create conflict and inefficiency.

Understanding and improving team dynamics is essential for achieving shared goals.

Why Team Dynamics Matter

A team with strong dynamics works harmoniously, leveraging diverse strengths. Poor dynamics, like unresolved conflict or unclear roles, can derail progress and morale.

For example:

- A sports team with excellent communication and trust outperforms one with internal conflicts, even if the players have similar skills.

Example: Solving a Workplace Problem

Suppose a team faces delays due to poor collaboration.

- Without Addressing Dynamics: Blame spreads, and productivity drops further.

- With Positive Dynamics: Open discussions clarify roles, resolve misunderstandings, and align efforts.

This fosters efficiency and mutual support.

How to Build Positive Team Dynamics

1. Clarify Roles and Responsibilities:

Ensure everyone understands their contributions to avoid overlap or gaps.

2. Promote Open Communication:

Encourage sharing ideas, concerns, and feedback respectfully.

3. Foster Trust and Respect:

Build an environment where team members feel valued and supported.

4. Resolve Conflicts Early:

Address disagreements constructively before they escalate.

5. Celebrate Successes:

Acknowledge achievements to strengthen morale and unity.

Everyday Example of Team Dynamics

Imagine organizing a community cleanup event.

- Positive Dynamics: Volunteers know their tasks, communicate clearly, and support one another, leading to a successful event.

This approach ensures smooth execution and satisfaction for everyone involved.

Common Pitfalls in Team Dynamics

1. Ignoring Group Conflicts:

Small disagreements can grow into major issues if left unaddressed.

2. Favoring Certain Members:

Unequal attention creates resentment and disrupts harmony.

3. Overlooking Individual Strengths:

Failing to recognize talents limits the team's potential.

4. Neglecting Inclusion:

Excluding quieter members stifles valuable contributions.

Practical Tip: Use Icebreakers and Team Activities

Regular team-building exercises enhance trust, communication, and understanding among members.

Takeaway

Team Dynamics shape the foundation of collaboration and success. By fostering trust, communication, and clarity, you create an environment where everyone thrives.

Chapter 90: Mentorship and Coaching

What are Mentorship and Coaching?

Mentorship and Coaching are relationships focused on personal and professional growth.

- **Mentorship:** A long-term relationship where an experienced person shares wisdom to guide a mentee.

- **Coaching:** A more structured, short-term approach to help individuals achieve specific goals.

Both are invaluable for skill development, confidence building, and achieving success.

Why Mentorship and Coaching Matter

Guidance from mentors and coaches accelerates learning, helping individuals navigate challenges and unlock their potential.

For example:

- A mentor helps a junior employee understand industry trends, while a coach supports them in developing time management skills.

Example: Advancing in a Career

Suppose you're transitioning to a leadership role.

- A Mentor: Shares lessons from their experience, helping you navigate new responsibilities.

- A Coach: Works with you to build specific skills like communication and decision-making.

Both approaches complement each other to ensure success.

How to Be an Effective Mentor or Coach

1. Build Trust:

Create a safe, supportive environment for open communication.

2. Listen Actively:

Understand the mentee's or coachee's goals, challenges, and aspirations.

3. Provide Constructive Feedback:

Offer insights that inspire growth while maintaining encouragement.

4. Set Clear Goals:

Collaborate on achievable objectives and actionable plans.

5. Celebrate Progress:

Acknowledge milestones to boost confidence and motivation.

Everyday Example of Mentorship

Imagine teaching a younger sibling how to manage finances.

- Mentor Role: Share personal experiences and lessons.

- Coach Role: Help them create a realistic budget and track progress.

This dual approach builds both knowledge and practical skills.

Common Pitfalls in Mentorship and Coaching

1. Imposing Personal Views:

Focus on guiding, not dictating, the individual's path.

2. Neglecting Boundaries:

Respect professional and personal limits within the relationship.

3. Overloading with Feedback:

Provide feedback in manageable, actionable steps.

4. Lacking Follow-Up:

Regular check-ins maintain momentum and accountability.

Practical Tip: Use SMART Goals in Coaching

Set Specific, Measurable, Achievable, Relevant, and Time-bound goals to guide progress effectively.

Takeaway

Mentorship and Coaching empower individuals by providing guidance, skills, and support tailored to their needs. These relationships are key to fostering growth and achieving goals.

Let's move on to productivity strategies.

Productivity and Self-Management Models

Chapter 91: The Pomodoro Technique

What is The Pomodoro Technique?

The Pomodoro Technique is a time-management method that divides work into focused intervals (usually 25 minutes), called "Pomodoros," followed by short breaks. This system helps maintain focus, prevent burnout, and boost productivity.

Why The Pomodoro Technique Matters

Long, uninterrupted work sessions can lead to fatigue and reduced efficiency. Pomodoros create a rhythm of intense focus and relaxation, improving overall output and reducing stress.

For example:

- A student uses Pomodoros to study for exams, completing sessions of focused reading with regular breaks to stay energized.

Example: Writing a Report

Suppose you need to draft a detailed report.

- Plan: Break the task into smaller sections (e.g., introduction, data analysis, conclusion).

- Pomodoros: Spend 25 minutes writing each section, with 5-minute breaks in between.

This approach keeps you motivated and prevents mental fatigue.

How to Use the Pomodoro Technique

1. Choose a Task:

Select a specific, measurable goal to focus on.

2. Set a Timer:

Work on the task for 25 minutes without distractions.

3. Take a Short Break:

Rest for 5 minutes to recharge.

4. Repeat the Cycle:

After four Pomodoros, take a longer break of 15–30 minutes.

5. Track Progress:

Note completed Pomodoros to measure productivity.

Everyday Example of the Pomodoro Technique

Imagine cleaning your house.

- Use Pomodoros to tackle one area (e.g., kitchen) for 25 minutes, then take a short break before moving to the next task.

This keeps chores manageable and prevents feeling overwhelmed.

Common Pitfalls in the Pomodoro Technique

1. Skipping Breaks:

Neglecting rest defeats the purpose of the technique.

2. Multitasking:

Focus on one task per Pomodoro for maximum effectiveness.

3. Underestimating Preparation Time:

Ensure you gather materials and plan tasks before starting.

4. Stopping Mid-Flow:

If deeply immersed, consider finishing your thought before the timer ends.

Practical Tip: Use Digital Pomodoro Apps

Apps and timers designed for the Pomodoro Technique simplify tracking and help you stay on schedule.

Takeaway

The Pomodoro Technique boosts productivity by balancing focus and relaxation. It's a simple yet powerful method for managing time effectively.

Chapter 92: SMART Goals

What are SMART Goals?

SMART Goals are a structured framework for setting clear, actionable objectives. Each goal is:

- **Specific:** Clearly defined and focused.

- **Measurable:** Quantifiable to track progress.

- **Achievable:** Realistic and attainable.

- **Relevant:** Aligned with broader priorities.

- **Time-bound:** Set within a defined timeframe.

This model ensures goals are practical and motivating.

Why SMART Goals Matter

Vague goals lead to confusion and lack of direction. SMART Goals provide clarity, accountability, and focus, increasing the likelihood of success.

For example:

- A vague goal: *"Get fit."*

- A SMART goal: *"Lose 10 pounds by exercising 4 times a week and tracking meals for 3 months."*

The SMART version is actionable and trackable.

Example: Career Advancement

Suppose you aim to develop professionally.

- SMART Goal: *"Complete a certification in project management within six months by studying 10 hours a week."*

This goal is specific, measurable, achievable, relevant, and time-bound, providing a clear path to achievement.

How to Create SMART Goals

1. Define the Goal:

Be as specific as possible.

2. Set Metrics:

Identify how you'll measure success (e.g., numbers, dates).

3. Assess Feasibility:

Ensure the goal is challenging yet realistic.

4. Align with Priorities:

Focus on goals that matter to your personal or professional growth.

5. Set Deadlines:

Break the goal into smaller milestones to stay on track.

Everyday Example of SMART Goals

Imagine planning a family vacation.

- Vague Goal: *"Plan a great trip."*
- SMART Goal: *"Book flights, accommodations, and activities for a weeklong trip to Paris by the end of the month."*

This approach ensures efficient and timely planning.

Common Pitfalls in SMART Goals

1. Being Overly Ambitious:

Goals should stretch your abilities without overwhelming you.

2. Skipping Metrics:

Without measurable criteria, progress becomes unclear.

3. Ignoring Relevance:

Pursuing unrelated goals diverts focus from your priorities.

4. Lacking Flexibility:

Adjust goals if circumstances change, maintaining their relevance.

Practical Tip: Review Goals Weekly

Regular check-ins ensure you stay on track and adapt as needed.

Takeaway

SMART Goals transform aspirations into actionable plans. This framework keeps you focused, motivated, and on course to achieve meaningful results.

Let's move on to time-management techniques.

Chapter 93: Pareto Time Management

What is Pareto Time Management?

Pareto Time Management applies the **Pareto Principle** (80/20 Rule) to productivity, suggesting that 80% of outcomes result from 20% of efforts. By identifying and focusing on high-impact tasks, you can achieve more with less effort.

Why Pareto Time Management Matters

Not all tasks are equal. Spending too much time on low-value activities wastes energy and reduces results. The Pareto Principle helps you prioritize efforts that yield the greatest benefits.

For example:

- A business owner may find that 80% of revenue comes from 20% of customers. Prioritizing these key clients maximizes profitability.

Example: Planning a Presentation

Suppose you're preparing for a presentation.

- Without Pareto: You spend hours perfecting minor details like font styles, ignoring the main content.

- With Pareto: You focus on crafting compelling arguments and visuals that deliver the most impact.

This approach ensures your effort translates into results.

How to Apply Pareto Time Management

1. Identify High-Value Tasks:

Determine which 20% of tasks contribute the most to your goals.

2. Focus on Prioritization:

Allocate the majority of your time and energy to these tasks.

3. Minimize Low-Impact Work:

Delegate or simplify less critical activities.

4. Evaluate Results Regularly:

Adjust your focus based on changing priorities or feedback.

Everyday Example of Pareto Time Management

Imagine cleaning your house before guests arrive.

- Pareto Approach: Focus on tidying visible areas like the living room and kitchen instead of organizing every closet.

This ensures you make the most noticeable improvements efficiently.

Common Pitfalls in Pareto Time Management

1. Misidentifying Key Tasks:

Spend time determining which tasks truly drive results.

2. Neglecting Less Urgent Work:

Some minor tasks still need occasional attention—don't ignore them entirely.

3. Getting Stuck in Details:

Avoid perfectionism when completing high-impact tasks.

4. Failing to Adapt:

Regularly reassess priorities as goals evolve.

Practical Tip: Use a Priority Matrix

Divide tasks into four categories: high value/high effort, high value/low effort, low value/high effort, and low value/low effort. Focus on the high-value tasks.

Takeaway

Pareto Time Management amplifies productivity by concentrating effort on what truly matters. It's a practical approach to maximizing impact with limited time.

Let's explore how to manage mental load and incomplete tasks.

Chapter 94: The Zeigarnik Effect

What is The Zeigarnik Effect?

The Zeigarnik Effect is the psychological tendency to remember incomplete tasks more vividly than completed ones. This effect often creates mental clutter but can also motivate you to finish what you start.

Why The Zeigarnik Effect Matters

Unfinished tasks weigh on your mind, causing stress and distraction. Recognizing this effect helps you manage mental load, prioritize work, and maintain focus.

For example:

- Leaving a report half-written may nag at you throughout the day, reducing concentration on other activities.

Example: Managing a To-Do List

Suppose you're juggling multiple projects.

- Without Awareness: You switch tasks frequently, leaving many unfinished and increasing stress.

- With Awareness: You tackle tasks one at a time, reducing the cognitive burden of incomplete work.

This strategy enhances focus and productivity.

How to Manage The Zeigarnik Effect

1. Break Tasks Into Steps:

Focus on completing small, manageable portions of a larger project.

2. Use To-Do Lists:

Track tasks to offload them from your mind and avoid forgetfulness.

3. Prioritize Completion:

Finish high-priority tasks before starting new ones.

4. Embrace Momentum:

Start tasks immediately to create a sense of progress.

Everyday Example of The Zeigarnik Effect

Imagine leaving an email draft unfinished.

- Effect: You keep thinking about it until it's sent.

- Solution: Finish the email immediately or schedule a time to complete it, reducing mental clutter.

This approach clears your mind and improves focus.

Common Pitfalls in Managing The Zeigarnik Effect

1. Procrastinating Starts:

Delaying tasks increases mental burden over time.

2. Overloading Yourself:

Taking on too many tasks amplifies the effect, creating overwhelm.

3. Ignoring Small Wins:

Celebrate completed steps to reduce the pressure of unfinished work.

4. Failing to Organize Tasks:

Unstructured workflows make it harder to track progress and completion.

Practical Tip: Use the "Two-Minute Rule"

If a task takes less than two minutes to complete, do it immediately to reduce mental clutter.

Takeaway

The Zeigarnik Effect highlights how unfinished tasks linger in your mind. Managing this effect helps you stay focused, reduce stress, and complete work efficiently.

Chapter 95: Energy Management

What is Energy Management?

Energy Management focuses on optimizing tasks based on your energy levels throughout the day. Unlike time management, which prioritizes hours, energy management ensures you tackle demanding tasks when you're most alert and save routine activities for low-energy periods.

Why Energy Management Matters

Productivity isn't just about time—it's about the quality of focus and effort. Recognizing your energy peaks and troughs allows you to work smarter, not harder.

For example:

- Writing a detailed report is easier during a high-energy period, while answering emails suits a low-energy phase.

Example: Planning Your Day

Suppose you're most energized in the morning.

- Without Energy Management: You use this time for minor tasks, leaving difficult work for the afternoon slump.

- With Energy Management: You schedule complex tasks for the morning and save simple ones for later.

This strategy maximizes both efficiency and satisfaction.

How to Manage Energy Effectively

1. Track Your Energy Levels:

Observe your energy patterns over several days to identify peaks and dips.

2. Schedule Around Peaks:

Assign challenging or creative tasks to high-energy periods.

3. Incorporate Breaks:

Short, regular breaks prevent burnout and restore energy.

4. Maintain Healthy Habits:

Prioritize sleep, nutrition, hydration, and exercise to sustain energy.

5. Batch Routine Tasks:

Group less demanding tasks for low-energy times.

Everyday Example of Energy Management

Imagine needing to study and do housework.

- Morning (High Energy): Focus on studying complex topics.

- Evening (Low Energy): Tackle housework while winding down.

This approach ensures both tasks are completed efficiently.

Common Pitfalls in Energy Management

1. Ignoring Energy Fluctuations:

Treating all hours equally reduces effectiveness.

2. Overloading Peak Times:

Avoid scheduling too many tasks during high-energy periods.

3. Skipping Breaks:

Prolonged effort without rest leads to exhaustion.

4. Underestimating Recovery:

Neglecting sleep and downtime depletes long-term energy reserves.

Practical Tip: Use Time Blocking

Divide your day into blocks for high, moderate, and low-energy tasks, aligning them with your natural rhythms.

Takeaway

Energy Management enhances productivity by aligning tasks with your energy levels. It's a powerful complement to time management for achieving sustainable performance.

Let's now explore how to streamline workflows and reduce multitasking.

Chapter 96: Task Batching

What is Task Batching?

Task Batching involves grouping similar tasks together and completing them in dedicated sessions. This approach minimizes context switching, which drains focus and productivity.

Why Task Batching Matters

Switching between unrelated tasks wastes mental energy and increases errors. Batching allows you to stay in a consistent workflow, boosting concentration and efficiency.

For example:

- Responding to all emails at once is faster and less disruptive than checking them sporadically throughout the day.

Example: Organizing Daily Tasks

Suppose you have emails, meetings, and creative writing to complete.

- Without Batching: You alternate between tasks, breaking focus repeatedly.

- With Batching: You designate blocks of time for each type of task, maintaining flow.

This approach improves both quality and speed.

How to Batch Tasks Effectively

1. Identify Similar Tasks:

Group tasks requiring similar tools or mindsets (e.g., phone calls, administrative work).

2. Create Dedicated Blocks:

Set specific times for each batch to maintain focus.

3. Eliminate Distractions:

Turn off notifications or block interruptions during batching sessions.

4. Stick to the Plan:

Avoid switching to unrelated tasks before completing the batch.

Everyday Example of Task Batching

Imagine managing your household responsibilities.

- Batch all errands like grocery shopping, post office trips, and bill payments into one outing instead of spreading them across the week.

This saves time and reduces repetitive effort.

Common Pitfalls in Task Batching

1. Overloading Batches:

Grouping too many tasks together overwhelms focus.

2. Failing to Prioritize:

Batching low-priority tasks wastes prime productivity hours.

3. Ignoring Breaks:

Long batching sessions without rest diminish quality.

4. Being Inflexible:

Allow room for urgent or unexpected tasks without derailing your schedule.

Practical Tip: Use Task Categories

Divide tasks into categories like "Quick Tasks," "Deep Work," and "Collaborative Work" to simplify batching.

Takeaway

Task Batching improves focus and efficiency by organizing similar tasks into dedicated sessions. It's a simple yet effective strategy for reducing mental fatigue and enhancing productivity.

Chapter 97: The Eisenhower Box

What is The Eisenhower Box?

The Eisenhower Box, or Matrix, is a decision-making framework that categorizes tasks based on their urgency and importance:

1. Urgent and Important: Do these immediately.

2. Not Urgent but Important: Schedule these for later.

3. Urgent but Not Important: Delegate these.

4. Not Urgent and Not Important: Eliminate these.

This model ensures focus on meaningful work while minimizing distractions.

Why The Eisenhower Box Matters

Many people confuse urgency with importance, wasting energy on tasks that don't align with their goals. This framework clarifies priorities and reduces stress.

For example:

- Responding to a client crisis is urgent and important, while checking social media is neither.

Example: Planning Your Week

Suppose you're overwhelmed by a long to-do list.

- **Urgent and Important:** Submit a project report due today.

- **Not Urgent but Important:** Start a fitness plan for long-term health.

- **Urgent but Not Important:** Respond to routine emails.

- **Not Urgent and Not Important:** Skip binge-watching a series.

Categorizing tasks ensures focus on what truly matters.

How to Use The Eisenhower Box

1. List All Tasks:

Write down everything you need to do.

2. Assign Categories:

Sort tasks into the four quadrants based on urgency and importance.

3. Act Accordingly:

Address tasks in order of priority: do, schedule, delegate, or eliminate.

4. Review Regularly:

Update the matrix as priorities change.

Everyday Example of The Eisenhower Box

Imagine managing household chores:

- Urgent and Important: Fixing a leaky faucet.

- Not Urgent but Important: Decluttering the attic.

- Urgent but Not Important: Answering a neighbor's non-urgent question.

- Not Urgent and Not Important: Rearranging decorative items.

This approach ensures efficient use of time and energy.

Common Pitfalls in Using The Eisenhower Box

1. Misclassifying Tasks:

Avoid overestimating urgency or importance.

2. Neglecting Scheduled Tasks:

Important but non-urgent tasks often get postponed—prioritize them.

3. Reluctance to Delegate:

Trust others to handle non-critical tasks.

4. Ignoring Unimportant Tasks:

Eliminate low-value tasks to free up mental space.

Practical Tip: Start Each Day with the Box

Begin your morning by reviewing and updating your Eisenhower Box to maintain focus.

Takeaway

The Eisenhower Box helps you prioritize effectively by distinguishing urgent tasks from important ones. It's a powerful tool for managing time and achieving meaningful goals.

Chapter 98: Mindfulness

What is Mindfulness?

Mindfulness is the practice of focusing on the present moment with full attention and without judgment. It involves being aware of your thoughts, feelings, and surroundings while maintaining a sense of calm and clarity.

Why Mindfulness Matters

Modern life is full of distractions and stressors that pull attention in many directions. Mindfulness reduces mental clutter, improves focus, and enhances emotional well-being.

For example:

- A mindful individual notices rising frustration during a tense conversation, pauses, and responds calmly instead of reacting impulsively.

Example: Staying Focused at Work

Suppose you're distracted by notifications while working.

- Without Mindfulness: You multitask, reducing the quality of your work.

- With Mindfulness: You silence distractions, focus fully on the task, and complete it more efficiently.

This approach boosts both productivity and satisfaction.

How to Practice Mindfulness

1. Start Small:

Spend 5–10 minutes daily focusing on your breath or observing your thoughts.

2. Engage Your Senses:

Notice the sights, sounds, and sensations around you to stay grounded.

3. Let Go of Judgments:

Accept thoughts and feelings as they arise without labeling them as good or bad.

4. Use Mindfulness Cues:

Associate mindfulness with daily activities like eating or walking to build consistency.

Everyday Example of Mindfulness

Imagine eating lunch.

- Without Mindfulness: You scroll through your phone, barely tasting the food.

- With Mindfulness: You savor each bite, notice textures and flavors, and feel more satisfied.

This practice transforms routine moments into sources of joy and calm.

Common Pitfalls in Mindfulness

1. Expecting Instant Results:

Mindfulness is a skill that grows with practice.

2. Overcomplicating the Practice:

Simplicity is key—focus on presence rather than perfection.

3. Judging Progress:

Avoid criticizing yourself for wandering thoughts.

4. Skipping Regular Practice:

Consistency is essential for reaping long-term benefits.

Practical Tip: Use Guided Meditations

Apps and videos offer structured mindfulness exercises for beginners and advanced practitioners alike.

Takeaway

Mindfulness enhances focus, reduces stress, and enriches everyday experiences. It's a simple yet transformative practice for improving both mental clarity and emotional balance.

Chapter 99: Decision Fatigue

What is Decision Fatigue?

Decision Fatigue occurs when the quality of decisions declines after making too many choices in a short period. Mental energy is a finite resource, and excessive decision-making drains it, leading to impulsive, delayed, or poor choices.

Why Decision Fatigue Matters

In a world filled with endless options, recognizing and managing decision fatigue helps conserve mental clarity for critical tasks.

For example:

- A manager who spends the morning on trivial decisions might struggle to focus on strategic choices later in the day.

Example: Grocery Shopping

Suppose you go to the store after a long day of meetings.

- Without Awareness: Decision fatigue leads to buying snacks impulsively instead of sticking to your list.

- With Awareness: You shop with a prepared list, reducing unnecessary choices.

This approach saves time, energy, and money.

How to Combat Decision Fatigue

1. Simplify Routine Choices:

Automate or pre-plan minor decisions like meals, outfits, or daily schedules.

2. Prioritize Important Decisions:

Tackle high-stakes choices early in the day when mental energy is highest.

3. Limit Options:

Narrow down choices to focus on the best options rather than endless possibilities.

4. Take Breaks:

Short rests or switching tasks refreshes your mind for better decision-making.

Everyday Example of Managing Decision Fatigue

Imagine planning your week.

- Effective Strategy: Use Sunday to create a weekly meal plan and prioritize key tasks.

- Result: Fewer daily decisions free mental energy for unexpected challenges.

This proactive approach reduces stress and improves outcomes.

Common Pitfalls in Decision Fatigue

1. Procrastinating Decisions:

Avoid delaying decisions, which compounds stress.

2. Overloading Choices:

Too many options create unnecessary mental strain.

3. Neglecting Self-Care:

Fatigue worsens without rest, proper nutrition, and hydration.

4. Ignoring Decision Quality:

Rushed choices often lead to mistakes or regret.

Practical Tip: Use Decision Frameworks

Rely on tools like the Eisenhower Box or pros-and-cons lists to streamline decision-making.

Takeaway

Decision Fatigue highlights the importance of conserving mental energy by simplifying, prioritizing, and pacing choices. Thoughtful management ensures better decisions and less stress.

Let's conclude with a practice for continuous improvement and self-awareness.

DAILY REVIEW

Chapter 100: Daily Review and Reflection

What is Daily Review and Reflection?

Daily Review and Reflection is the practice of evaluating your actions, accomplishments, and lessons each day. This habit promotes self-awareness, gratitude, and continuous improvement.

Why Daily Review and Reflection Matter

Pausing to assess your day helps reinforce positive habits, identify areas for growth, and maintain alignment with your long-term goals.

For example:

- Reflecting on a productive meeting helps you understand what worked and replicate it in future discussions.

Example: Reflecting on a Busy Day

Suppose you had a day filled with highs and lows.

- Review: Identify three things that went well and one area needing improvement.

- Plan: Use these insights to set actionable goals for tomorrow.

This practice ensures consistent progress and growth.

How to Practice Daily Review and Reflection

1. Set Aside Time:

Dedicate 5–10 minutes at the end of each day for reflection.

2. Use a Simple Structure:

Divide your review into categories like achievements, challenges, and lessons.

3. Celebrate Small Wins:

Acknowledge progress, no matter how minor, to boost motivation.

4. Plan Ahead:

Set one or two priorities for the next day based on your reflections.

Everyday Example of Daily Review

Imagine preparing for bed.

- Reflect: Think about a kind act you did, a mistake you can learn from, and one thing you're grateful for.

This practice fosters positivity and self-awareness.

Common Pitfalls in Daily Review and Reflection

1. Being Overly Critical:

Focus on learning from mistakes, not dwelling on them.

2. Skipping Consistency:

Regular reflection is key to building habits and tracking progress.

3. Ignoring Emotional Aspects:

Consider how actions or events made you feel, not just outcomes.

4. Setting Unrealistic Goals:

Break large goals into smaller, actionable steps to maintain momentum.

Practical Tip: Use Journaling Prompts

Daily prompts like *"What did I learn today?"* or *"What's one thing I'm proud of?"* make reflection easier and more meaningful.

Takeaway

Daily Review and Reflection create a cycle of learning, gratitude, and growth. This simple yet powerful practice ensures steady improvement and alignment with your values and goals.

Conclusion: Mastering Mental Models for Lifelong Success

Congratulations!

You've reached the end of an incredible journey through 100 mental models designed to sharpen your thinking, clarify your decision-making, and amplify your understanding of the world. From simplifying problems with Occam's Razor to navigating complex systems with Systems Thinking, you've equipped yourself with tools to approach challenges in smarter, more thoughtful ways.

These mental models aren't just theories—they're practical strategies for everyday life. Whether you're planning your day, analyzing risks, or solving intricate problems, these models provide a framework to think critically, act decisively, and grow consistently.

What Comes Next?

Mental models are like muscles — the more you use them, the stronger they get. Practice applying these tools to your decisions, your conversations, and your reflections. You'll find they become second nature over time, helping you see patterns, simplify complexity, and make better choices.

If you enjoyed this journey, I'd be thrilled to hear your thoughts! Share a review or recommendation — it's like telling a friend about a great idea. And remember, there's always more to explore. From bias-busting techniques to advanced decision-making frameworks, this is just the start of what you can discover.

Key Takeaways for the Road:

1. Stay Curious: Keep asking questions and challenging assumptions.

2. Embrace Clarity: Break problems into smaller parts and focus on core truths.

3. Think Holistically: Always consider how small decisions impact the bigger picture.

4. Adapt and Reflect: Learn from mistakes and refine your approach as you go.

Armed with these tools, you're ready to engage with the world in a deeper, more intentional way. Here's to smarter decisions, clearer thinking, and a future filled with possibilities!

Appendix A: Quick Reference Guide to 100 Mental Models

This appendix offers a concise description of all 100 mental models, making it easy to refresh your understanding or apply the right model in various scenarios.

1–10: Foundational Thinking Models

1. Occam's Razor: Choose the simplest explanation with the fewest assumptions.

2. First Principles Thinking: Break problems into basic elements and rebuild from the ground up.

3. Second-Order Thinking: Consider long-term consequences and ripple effects of actions.

4. Hanlon's Razor: Assume ignorance over malice when interpreting misunderstandings.

5. Inversion: Think about the opposite outcome to identify risks and opportunities.

6. Probabilistic Thinking: Use probabilities to guide decisions in uncertain situations.

7. Bayesian Thinking: Update beliefs based on new evidence to better align with reality.

8. Systems Thinking: Recognize how elements in a system interact and influence the whole.

9. Compound Interest: Understand how consistent growth builds exponentially over time.

10. Circle of Competence: Focus on areas of expertise and expand your knowledge incrementally.

11–20: Learning and Adaptability Models

11. The Learning Curve: Efficiency improves with practice and repetition.

12. Feedback Loops: Use feedback—positive or negative—to refine processes and results.

13. Meta-Learning: Master the art of learning itself by identifying effective strategies.

14. Incremental Growth: Make small, continuous improvements to achieve long-term success.

15. Shoshin (Beginner's Mind): Approach situations with curiosity and openness, even as an expert.

16. Agility in Learning: Adapt quickly to new information or unexpected challenges.

17. Mental Flexibility: Consider multiple perspectives and avoid rigid thinking.

18. Self-Reflection: Analyze past actions to improve future decisions and behavior.

19. Failure Analysis: Treat mistakes as opportunities to grow and improve.

20. Challenge Bias: Actively seek out evidence that contradicts your current beliefs.

21–30: Decision-Making Models

21. Cost-Benefit Analysis: Weigh the pros and cons to choose the most advantageous option.

22. Expected Value: Evaluate potential outcomes by considering probabilities and impacts.

23. Opportunity Cost: Factor in what is sacrificed when choosing one option over another.

24. Pareto Principle (80/20 Rule): Focus on the small percentage of efforts that yield the largest results.

25. Marginal Utility: Understand how the value of resources diminishes as consumption increases.

26. Loss Aversion: Recognize our tendency to avoid losses more strongly than pursuing equivalent gains.

27. The Eisenhower Matrix: Prioritize tasks based on urgency and importance to manage time effectively.

28. SWOT Analysis: Assess Strengths, Weaknesses, Opportunities, and Threats for decision-making.

29. Decision Trees: Map out options and their potential consequences to clarify complex choices.

30. Game Theory: Evaluate choices in situations where outcomes depend on others' decisions.

31. Root Cause Analysis: Identify the fundamental reason behind an issue or failure.

32. 5 Whys Technique: Ask "Why?" repeatedly to uncover the underlying cause of a problem.

33. Lateral Thinking: Approach problems creatively, breaking away from traditional patterns.

34. The Feynman Technique: Simplify complex concepts by explaining them in plain language.

35. Heuristic Problem Solving: Use rules of thumb to make quick, practical decisions.

36. The Scientific Method: Form hypotheses, test them, and observe results systematically.

37. Abductive Reasoning: Seek the most likely explanation for a given set of observations.

38. Design Thinking: Focus on user-centric solutions through empathy, ideation, and iteration.

39. Hypothesis Testing: Experiment with assumptions to validate or disprove ideas.

40. A/B Testing: Compare two options in controlled trials to determine the best outcome.

41–50: Strategic Thinking Models

41. The OODA Loop: Observe, Orient, Decide, and Act to respond effectively to challenges.

42. Scenario Planning: Prepare for multiple future scenarios by envisioning possible outcomes.

43. The Hedgehog Concept: Focus on the intersection of passion, skill, and impact for sustained success.

44. Risk Management: Balance potential risks and rewards to make informed decisions.

45. Competitive Analysis: Evaluate the strengths and weaknesses of competitors to improve your strategy.

46. Red Teaming: Challenge ideas by viewing them from an adversarial or critical perspective.

47. Asymmetric Thinking: Use unconventional actions to achieve outsized results.

48. Crowdsourcing Ideas: Gather diverse input to generate innovative solutions.

49. Long-Term Thinking: Focus on sustainability and future impact rather than immediate gains.

50. Contingency Planning: Develop backup plans to handle unexpected events.

51–60: Communication Models

51. The 5W Model: Clarify communication by addressing Who, What, Where, When, and Why.

52. Active Listening: Focus fully on the speaker's words, tone, and intent without judgment.

53. Feedback Framework: Deliver constructive feedback that is actionable and encouraging.

54. Empathy Mapping: Visualize others' thoughts, feelings, and needs to improve communication.

55. The Elevator Pitch: Present ideas succinctly and persuasively in a short timeframe.

56. The Pyramid Principle: Organize arguments by starting with the conclusion and supporting details.

57. Storytelling: Use relatable narratives to simplify and convey complex ideas.

58. The 7 Cs of Communication: Ensure clarity, conciseness, and coherence in your messages.

59. Reframing: Change perspectives to see problems or solutions differently.

60. The Socratic Method: Ask probing questions to deepen understanding and uncover truths.

61–70: Behavioral and Cognitive Models

61. Cognitive Bias Awareness: Recognize and counteract biases that distort thinking.

62. Anchoring Bias: Avoid relying too heavily on the first piece of information received.

63. Confirmation Bias: Resist the urge to seek information that only supports your current beliefs.

64. Availability Heuristic: Recognize the tendency to overvalue recent or vivid experiences.

65. Social Proof: Understand how peer behavior influences decisions and actions.

66. Habit Formation: Build consistent, positive behaviors through repetition and cues.

67. Pavlovian Conditioning: Recognize how triggers influence responses and behaviors.

68. Emotional Regulation: Manage emotions to maintain clarity and improve decisions.

69. Self-Fulfilling Prophecy: Be aware of how expectations shape outcomes.

70. Grit and Resilience: Develop mental endurance to overcome challenges and pursue goals.

71-80: Financial and Economic Models

71. Supply and Demand: Understanding price and availability.

72. Sunk Cost Fallacy: Ignoring unrecoverable past investments.

73. Scarcity Principle: Recognizing limited resources increase value.

74. Risk-Reward Ratio: Balancing potential returns against risks.

75. The Law of Diminishing Returns: Understanding limits to productivity.

76. ROI (Return on Investment): Evaluating returns relative to cost.

77. Leverage: Using resources to amplify outcomes.

78. The Time Value of Money: Valuing money today over future money.

79. Arbitrage: Taking advantage of price differences in markets.

80. Budgeting and Forecasting: Planning financial resources.

81-90: Leadership and Influence Models

81. Servant Leadership: Prioritizing team needs over individual power.

82. Transactional vs. Transformational Leadership: Balancing routine and innovation.

83. The Peter Principle: Avoiding promotion beyond competence.

84. Emotional Intelligence: Understanding and managing emotions.

85. Influence Strategies: Using persuasion techniques effectively.

86. Conflict Resolution: Handling disagreements productively.

87. Delegation: Assigning tasks based on skills and interests.

88. Situational Leadership: Adapting style to the situation.

89. Team Dynamics: Understanding roles within group settings.

90. Mentorship and Coaching: Guiding others through shared wisdom.

91-100: Productivity and Self-Management Models

91. The Pomodoro Technique: Time-blocking for focus.

92. SMART Goals: Setting specific, measurable, achievable, relevant, and time-bound goals.

93. Pareto Time Management: Focusing on tasks with the biggest impact.

94. The Zeigarnik Effect: Noting tasks to reduce mental load.

95. Energy Management: Prioritizing high-energy times for hard tasks.

96. Task Batching: Grouping similar tasks for efficiency.

97. The Eisenhower Box: Sorting tasks by urgency and importance.

98. Mindfulness: Maintaining focus on the present.

99. Decision Fatigue: Minimizing choices to conserve mental energy.

100. Daily Review and Reflection: Evaluating each day to improve habits.

Appendix B: Mental Models by Category

This appendix organizes all 100 mental models into intuitive categories, making it easier to find the tools you need for specific challenges.

Foundational Thinking Models

- Occam's Razor
- First Principles Thinking
- Second-Order Thinking
- Hanlon's Razor
- Inversion
- Probabilistic Thinking
- Bayesian Thinking
- Systems Thinking
- Compound Interest
- Circle of Competence

Learning and Adaptability Models

- The Learning Curve
- Feedback Loops
- Meta-Learning
- Incremental Growth
- Shoshin (Beginner's Mind)
- Agility in Learning
- Mental Flexibility
- Self-Reflection
- Failure Analysis
- Challenge Bias

Decision-Making Models

- Cost-Benefit Analysis
- Expected Value
- Opportunity Cost
- Pareto Principle (80/20 Rule)
- Marginal Utility
- Loss Aversion
- The Eisenhower Matrix
- SWOT Analysis
- Decision Trees
- Game Theory

Problem-Solving Models

- Root Cause Analysis

- 5 Whys Technique

- Lateral Thinking

- The Feynman Technique

- Heuristic Problem Solving

- The Scientific Method

- Abductive Reasoning

- Design Thinking

- Hypothesis Testing

- A/B Testing

Strategic Thinking Models

- The OODA Loop

- Scenario Planning

- The Hedgehog Concept

- Risk Management

- Competitive Analysis

- Red Teaming

- Asymmetric Thinking

- Crowdsourcing Ideas

- Long-Term Thinking

- Contingency Planning

Communication Models

- The 5W Model

- Active Listening

- Feedback Framework

- Empathy Mapping

- The Elevator Pitch

- The Pyramid Principle

- Storytelling

- The 7 Cs of Communication

- Reframing

- The Socratic Method

Behavioral and Cognitive Models

- Cognitive Bias Awareness

- Anchoring Bias

- Confirmation Bias

- Availability Heuristic

- Social Proof

- Habit Formation

- Pavlovian Conditioning

- Emotional Regulation

- Self-Fulfilling Prophecy

- Grit and Resilience

Financial and Economic Models

- Supply and Demand
- Sunk Cost Fallacy
- Scarcity Principle
- Risk-Reward Ratio
- The Law of Diminishing Returns
- ROI (Return on Investment)
- Leverage
- The Time Value of Money
- Arbitrage
- Budgeting and Forecasting

Leadership and Influence Models

- Servant Leadership
- Transactional vs. Transformational Leadership
- The Peter Principle
- Emotional Intelligence
- Influence Strategies
- Conflict Resolution
- Delegation
- Situational Leadership
- Team Dynamics
- Mentorship and Coaching

Productivity and Self-Management Models

- The Pomodoro Technique

- SMART Goals

- Pareto Time Management

- The Zeigarnik Effect

- Energy Management

- Task Batching

- The Eisenhower Box

- Mindfulness

- Decision Fatigue

- Daily Review and Reflection

Appendix C: Practice Scenarios – Applying Mental Models

Use the following scenarios to test your understanding of mental models and practice applying them in real-life situations. Each example is followed by the appropriate model(s) to apply and a brief explanation to guide your thought process.

Scenario 1: Project Overload

You're a team leader managing three critical projects, but your team is feeling overwhelmed by the workload. You need to decide which project should take priority to ensure success.

- **Models to Apply:** Pareto Principle, Eisenhower Matrix

- **Solution:** Use the Pareto Principle to identify which project delivers the most value (the 20% driving 80% of results). Then, apply the Eisenhower Matrix to prioritize tasks within the project based on urgency and importance.

Scenario 2: Unexpected Market Changes

Your business faces new competition in a rapidly shifting market. You must decide how to adapt your strategy to maintain your competitive edge.

- **Models to Apply:** Scenario Planning, SWOT Analysis, Red Teaming

- **Solution:** Use Scenario Planning to evaluate possible future changes in the market and how they might affect your business. SWOT Analysis will help identify your business's strengths, weaknesses, opportunities, and threats. Finally, Red Teaming can challenge your current strategies by assessing them from an adversarial perspective.

Scenario 3: Simplifying a Complex Problem

Your team struggles to understand why a product launch failed. The reasons seem endless and overwhelming, leaving you unsure where to start solving the issue.

- **Models to Apply:** First Principles Thinking, Root Cause Analysis, 5 Whys Technique

- **Solution:** Break the problem into fundamental elements using First Principles Thinking. Then, conduct Root Cause Analysis by asking "Why?" repeatedly (5 Whys Technique) to drill down to the core issue causing the failure.

Scenario 4: Personal Budget Management

You're trying to save money for a big vacation, but you're not sure where to cut expenses without impacting your lifestyle too much.

- **Models to Apply:** Opportunity Cost, Marginal Utility, Compound Interest

- **Solution:** Assess Opportunity Costs by evaluating what you gain or lose from each expense. Use Marginal Utility to prioritize spending on what brings the most value. Apply Compound Interest by investing small amounts now to grow savings over time.

Scenario 5: Miscommunication in the Workplace

A heated disagreement arises during a meeting because two team members have different interpretations of the project's goals. The tension is affecting morale.

- **Models to Apply:** Empathy Mapping, Reframing, Active Listening

- **Solution:** Use Empathy Mapping to understand each person's perspective and motivations. Reframe the disagreement by focusing on shared goals rather than differences. Practice Active Listening to ensure both parties feel heard and understood.

Scenario 6: Choosing a Career Path

You're considering two potential career paths: one is stable but unexciting, while the other is riskier but aligns more closely with your passions.

- **Models to Apply:** Circle of Competence, Decision Trees, Expected Value

- **Solution:** Assess each career path relative to your Circle of Competence to ensure you leverage your strengths. Use a Decision Tree to map out the potential outcomes of each choice. Apply Expected Value to weigh the potential risks and rewards of the riskier option.

Scenario 7: Delegating Tasks Effectively

You're managing a small team and struggling to delegate tasks without micromanaging or losing control of outcomes.

- **Models to Apply:** Delegation, Feedback Framework, Situational Leadership

- **Solution:** Use Delegation to assign tasks based on team members' strengths. Provide clear, actionable feedback using the Feedback Framework. Adapt your leadership style (Situational Leadership) to each team member's skill level and confidence.

Scenario 8: Learning a New Skill

You want to learn a new skill but feel overwhelmed by the complexity of the topic. You're unsure where to begin.

- **Models to Apply:** Incremental Growth, Meta-Learning, Shoshin (Beginner's Mind)

- **Solution:** Break the skill into smaller, manageable components (Incremental Growth). Study learning techniques specific to the skill (Meta-Learning). Adopt a Beginner's Mind to stay open to new concepts and avoid discouragement.

Scenario 9: Evaluating a Risky Investment

A friend suggests investing in a new startup. It could yield high returns, but there's significant uncertainty.

- **Models to Apply:** Risk Management, Bayesian Thinking, Probabilistic Thinking

- **Solution:** Use Risk Management to weigh potential rewards against risks. Apply Bayesian Thinking to update your decision as you gather more information about the startup. Use Probabilistic Thinking to consider the likelihood of success based on available data.

Scenario 10: Overcoming Procrastination

You keep putting off a large project because it feels overwhelming and unclear where to start.

- **Models to Apply:** Pomodoro Technique, Energy Management, Task Batching

- **Solution:** Break the project into smaller sessions using the Pomodoro Technique. Schedule challenging tasks during your peak energy times (Energy Management). Batch similar tasks to maintain focus and efficiency (Task Batching).

Appendix D: Mental Model Checklist

This checklist helps you apply mental models effectively when solving problems or making decisions. Use it as a step-by-step guide in any situation.

1. Defining and Clarifying the Problem

- **First Principles Thinking:** Have I stripped the problem down to its most basic elements?

- **Root Cause Analysis:** Have I identified the underlying reason for the issue rather than just treating symptoms?

- **5 Whys Technique:** Have I asked "Why?" multiple times to drill down to the core problem?

- **Shoshin (Beginner's Mind):** Am I approaching the problem with an open mind, free of assumptions?

2. Simplifying Complexity

- **Occam's Razor:** Am I choosing the simplest explanation that requires the fewest assumptions?

- **Reframing:** Have I considered different ways to view or define the problem?

- **Lateral Thinking:** Am I exploring unconventional or creative approaches to solving this issue?

3. Considering Broader Implications

- **Second-Order Thinking:** Have I thought about the ripple effects of my decision?

- **Systems Thinking:** Have I considered how this problem fits into the broader system and how changes might affect other parts?

- **Scenario Planning:** Have I planned for multiple possible outcomes or future scenarios?

4. Evaluating Trade-offs and Options

- **Pareto Principle:** Am I focusing on the 20% of efforts that will yield 80% of the results?

- **Opportunity Cost:** What am I giving up by pursuing this option? Is there a better use of my time or resources?

- **Expected Value:** Have I considered the probabilities and potential payoffs of each option?

5. Managing Priorities

- **Eisenhower Matrix:** Have I prioritized tasks based on urgency and importance?

- **Task Batching:** Have I grouped similar tasks together to work more efficiently?

- **Energy Management:** Am I scheduling high-priority tasks during my peak energy periods?

6. Using Data and Evidence

- **Bayesian Thinking:** Have I updated my beliefs with the most recent and relevant evidence?

- **Probabilistic Thinking:** Have I used probabilities to guide my decision-making in uncertain situations?

- **Feedback Loops:** Am I incorporating feedback to refine my approach and stay adaptable?

7. Learning and Growing

- **The Learning Curve:** Am I giving myself time to improve through practice and repetition?

- **Meta-Learning:** Am I using the most effective strategies to learn and grow?

- **Incremental Growth:** Am I focusing on small, consistent improvements instead of trying to achieve perfection all at once?

8. Making Decisions Strategically

- **Cost-Benefit Analysis:** Have I weighed the benefits and costs of each decision?

- **Game Theory:** Have I considered how others' decisions and actions might influence my outcomes?

- **SWOT Analysis:** Have I evaluated strengths, weaknesses, opportunities, and threats in this situation?

9. Reflecting on Actions and Outcomes

- **Daily Review and Reflection:** Am I taking time to assess what worked, what didn't, and why?

- **Failure Analysis:** What can I learn from any mistakes or setbacks?

- **Self-Reflection:** Am I regularly analyzing my choices to identify areas for improvement?

10. Overcoming Mental Barriers

- **Cognitive Bias Awareness:** Am I aware of biases like anchoring, confirmation bias, or loss aversion that might distort my thinking?

- **Loss Aversion:** Am I overly focused on avoiding losses rather than pursuing meaningful gains?

- **Emotional Regulation:** Am I making decisions calmly, without being overwhelmed by emotions?

11. Communicating Effectively

- **Empathy Mapping:** Have I considered how others might feel, think, and perceive the situation?

- **The Pyramid Principle:** Am I presenting my ideas logically, starting with the conclusion and building on it with supporting details?

- **Active Listening:** Am I fully engaged in understanding the perspectives of others before responding?

12. Thinking Creatively

- **Design Thinking:** Am I considering the needs of others to create user-centered solutions?

- **The Feynman Technique:** Can I explain the concept or problem in simple terms to ensure I truly understand it?

- **Lateral Thinking:** Am I challenging conventional methods and looking for alternative approaches?

13. Managing Long-Term Goals

- **Long-Term Thinking:** Am I making decisions with future sustainability and impact in mind?

- **Compound Interest:** Am I leveraging consistent small efforts to achieve exponential growth over time?

- **Circle of Competence:** Am I focusing on areas where I have expertise while gradually expanding my knowledge?

14. Evaluating Risks and Uncertainty

- **Risk Management:** Have I assessed the potential risks and rewards of each option?

- **Contingency Planning:** Have I prepared backup plans to handle unexpected challenges?

- **Marginal Utility:** Am I considering diminishing returns on effort or resources?

15. Building Resilience and Grit

- **Grit and Resilience:** Am I staying determined and adaptable in the face of challenges?

- **Self-Fulfilling Prophecy:** Am I fostering positive expectations to improve outcomes?

- **Shoshin (Beginner's Mind):** Am I remaining open to new possibilities, even when things seem difficult?

Keep this checklist handy to incorporate mental models into your daily decision-making process.

Here's another book by Quinn Voss that you might like

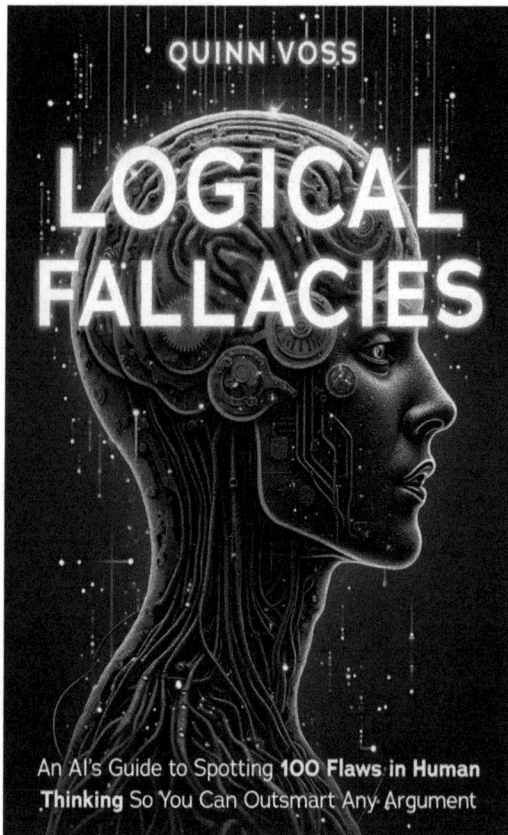

QUINN VOSS

LOGICAL FALLACIES

An AI's Guide to Spotting **100 Flaws in Human Thinking** So You Can Outsmart Any Argument

www.ingramcontent.com/pod-product-compliance
Lightning Source LLC
Chambersburg PA
CBHW070051030426

42335CB00016B/1848